SUPERTRAITS *of* SUPERSTARS

Priyanka Sinha Jha is a journalist who, in her eighteen-year-long career, has written on celebrities, films, lifestyle, business and more. She has been a correspondent for publications as varied as *Citadel, The Asian Age* and *Intelligent Investor*. At the age of twenty-six, she became the editor of *Society*, India's first celebrity magazine, followed by a stint as editor of *HT Style* and *HT Saturday*. Currently, she is the editor of *Screen*, India's foremost film and entertainment weekly. She has also contributed to *Outlook, The Week* and *Tehelka*, and has a regular column in *The Indian Express: Play*.

Between analysing celebrities and earning her daily bread, she likes to travel to unknown destinations, watch films and argue endlessly on egalitarian issues with friends and family.

SUPERTRAITS of SUPERSTARS

Success Secrets of Bollywood's Brightest

PRIYANKA SINHA JHA

RUPA

First published by
Rupa Publications India Pvt. Ltd 2014
7/16, Ansari Road, Daryaganj
New Delhi 110002

Sales Centres:

Allahabad Bengaluru Chennai
Hyderabad Jaipur Kathmandu
Kolkata Mumbai

Copyright © Priyanka Sinha Jha 2014
Illustrations copyright © K. Aishwarya 2014

All rights reserved.
No part of this publication may be reproduced, transmitted,
or stored in a retrieval system, in any form or by any means,
electronic, mechanical, photocopying, recording or otherwise,
without the prior permission of the publisher.

ISBN: 978-81-291-2978-9

First impression 2014

10 9 8 7 6 5 4 3 2 1

The moral right of the author has been asserted.

Printed by Manipal Technologies Ltd, Manipal

This book is sold subject to the condition that it shall not,
by way of trade or otherwise, be lent, resold, hired out, or otherwise
circulated, without the publisher's prior consent, in any form of binding or
cover other than that in which it is published.

Introduction

One of the first questions that family and friends-at-large posed when I told them about *Supertraits of Superstars* was: 'How come *you're* writing an inspirational book?'

The question was valid—I am not a life-coach, nor a motivational speaker. I have not conquered Mount Everest either.

The answer to that existential query has two parts. The first lies in my past and the second in my present.

As a child, it took me a really long time to find my space in the world. A good part of my childhood was spent with grandparents before I left for boarding school. Being a very sickly child, I missed out on school pretty often. I was an average student, none too good at extracurricular activities, and given my constant illness, I failed to make a mark. I was also painfully shy yet brutally frank; neither attribute of help in climbing the popularity charts. Being perceived as dull because I was shy or rude because of my extreme candour was obviously not doing much for my self-esteem.

Soon, daydreaming about beautiful places, where fairies set things right and nobody picked on tongue-tied kids by tagging them as dumb, turned into a habit. Lessons were neglected, and after my early indignation about the world being an unfair place, I settled into that comfortable zone, which children deemed mediocre are consigned to.

Perhaps this dull existence would have continued uninterrupted if I had not chanced upon a book called *Illusions* by Richard Bach. When I opened it, the first line that leaped out at me was, '...*you are never given a wish without the power to make it true...*'

It seemed as if there was some invisible hand—much like those imaginary fairies—pointing out the words to me. Suffice to say, the line made quite an impression and has stayed with me ever since. I suddenly felt empowered; it was as though the words had energized and transformed me from a 'poor dear' to someone who could seize the reins of her life and take charge.

My self-help journey had begun. It was a small step, but the positivity of those words gave me courage and the resolve to take control of my destiny. I began to look beyond disparaging faculty members and patronizing acquaintances for inspiration. A book on the French scientist Madame Marie Curie, given by my father, was the next inspirational read, followed by a cover interview of India's first woman IPS officer Kiran Bedi in *Savvy*, a leading women's magazine. These people and the trajectory of their lives altered my views of the world around me, and my self-expectations. They also threw into sharp relief the power of role models, both good and bad, and helped me find my own self.

And so I come to the present. In what can best be put down to serendipity, for the past decade, my line of work has involved writing extensively on celebrities at large and Bollywood actors in particular. To meet so many exceptional people, all in a lifetime, has been wonderful. Of course, the corollary to this

To Lord Ganesha, the lord of auspicious beginnings, the remover of obstacles, who carried me through this journey.

To Sita Sinha (Amma) and Janardan Prasad Sinha (Nanaji), who always urged me to pursue knowledge and goodness above all else.

To my husband Piyush, who helped me navigate my thoughts and shape them into Supertraits of Superstars.

Contents

Introduction ix

AMITABH BACHCHAN: Discipline 1

SHAH RUKH KHAN: Passion 19

VIDYA BALAN: Reinvention 39

AAMIR KHAN: Pursuit of Perfection 55

KATRINA KAIF: Perseverance 71

JOHN ABRAHAM: Enterprise 85

RANBIR RAJ KAPOOR: Maximal Focus 101

AISHWARYA RAI BACHCHAN: Grace under Pressure 117

HRITHIK ROSHAN: Overcoming the Achilles' Heel 135

KARAN JOHAR: Diplomacy and Tact 149

SALMAN KHAN: Generosity 165

Acknowledgements 182
References 184

blessing is that I am quizzed on the minutest details of their lives. After all, everybody wants a film-star lifestyle. We look to Bollywood stars for many things—success, money and fame—but to see them only as immensely wealthy or as famous people leading a charmed life would be a fraction of the truth. Many of us (and I ashamedly include myself) have been guilty of trash-talking film celebrities and summarily dismissing their accomplishments, but after observing them from close quarters, I have found a few of them truly admirable and inspiring. On several occasions, they have even been the beacons of light who have helped me tide over tricky situations.

These interactions led me to wonder about the motivation that drives some of the most successful Bollywood icons. I mulled over the question for a while; after all, success can be as difficult to process and assimilate as failure and rejection. And much like the rest of us, superstars too go through their share of heartbreaks, betrayal and harsh criticism. With the additional pressure of having to cope with it in full public view. A messy divorce, an ugly break-up, being thrown out of a film, financial troubles—they face it all, under our collective gaze.

The answer to the question of what drives them was slightly different from what I'd imagined it to be. Let's face it, besides being a highly demanding job, there are constant comparisons and speculations about the new kid on the block, who is the fairest of them all, who is the highest paid; it takes more than plain luck to achieve super success. It requires nerves of steel and, yes, definitive characteristics that collectively constitute an overriding supertrait to survive stardom.

And so was born the idea of an inspirational book citing examples of the distinctive supertraits of film stars.

I have drawn attention to eleven superstars, all with defining supertraits that have pole-vaulted them into the league of the extraordinary. These men and women have either honed a particular quality they possess to remarkable levels, working it to their advantage, or have, over time, displayed an ability to adapt, learn and land on their feet, even in extreme circumstances. The quotes of these superstars are culled from interviews and articles that have appeared over a period of time in print, television and websites (a majority of them are from interviews I have conducted for *Screen*).

The supertraits they possess are no boon from the gods. They have been sharpened patiently over years, even when the impulse may have been to just give up and run for dear life. Amitabh Bachchan (a prominent presence in this book) has often quoted his father, the eminent poet Harivansh Rai Bachchan's words, *'Jab tak jeevan hai, tab tak sangharsh hai.'* (While there is life, there is struggle.) It is also true that all of them possess some, if not all, of the other supertraits highlighted in this book, in varying degrees. But, like in the movies, I have kept to the main, defining trait of each actor in focus, leaving the rest in shadows.

The choice of names is very personal and therefore subjective; they are people who, in the course of professional interactions over the years (as the editor of *Screen* and earlier as the editor of *Hindustan Times Style*, *HT Saturday*, and *Society*) have influenced my thinking and approach to life in ways big and small. They have, on several occasions, unknowingly helped me help myself.

I must confess, though, that not all the supertraits mentioned in this book have been incorporated in my life as yet. But on the occasions that I have applied them, they have worked in my favour. For instance, though fairly disciplined on the work front, I have a long way to go in personal matters. I still need to work on making time for family dinners, achieving a greater stillness of mind, or not letting negativity get the better of me. Awareness, as they say, is merely the starting point; execution is lifelong. Quite like the lives of these superstars, acquiring supertraits is a work-in-progress at all times.

The heroes and sheroes (she-heroes) featured in this book—Amitabh Bachchan, Shah Rukh Khan, Aishwarya Rai Bachchan or Vidya Balan, to name just a few—while not perfect, are all exceptional for having survived the odds with such splendour. As Shah Rukh Khan says, 'Perfection is not inspiring, overcoming your own imperfections is.'

Supertraits of Superstars, based on observations and conversations with the superstars in question, besides other members from the film fraternity, comes from the vantage point of an outsider. It is an earnest tribute to Bollywood and the power of film stars.

While this book may or may not turn you into a Bollywood star, it can certainly make you a superstar in your own universe.

AMITABH BACHCHAN
Discipline

'Discipline is the bridge between goals and accomplishment.'

—Jim Rohn

A film premiere in New York, a red-carpet appearance at Cannes, in conversation with Hollywood director and producer Steven Spielberg in Mumbai or British Premiere David Cameron... But there's more: an appointment with designer Christian Louboutin, magazine shoots interspersed with daily blogging, catching up with his extended family of over sixty lakh followers on Twitter and more than fifty lakh fans on Facebook (at the last count), plus the multitudes who follow his blogs. All this besides television commitments, shooting for commercials, receiving innumerable awards, attending conclaves, music launches...the list could go on and on.

An average week in the life of Amitabh Bachchan packs in enough activities to last one a lifetime. The million-dollar question is—*how* does he manage to pull it off? The key lies in his unwavering discipline. Bachchan's discipline and ability to multitask with such felicity is both admirable and awe-inspiring. Considering that the superstar is the tallest of the living legends of Indian cinema, the frenetic schedule is understandable. It is his smooth execution that is nothing short of mind-boggling.

After over forty-four years in the industry and more than two hundred films, first as a newcomer,

Ek yantra banaya gaya hai jise ghadi kehte hain. Main usey dekh kar samay se pahunch jaata hoon.

then as a reigning superstar and now as living legend, Bachchan has ridden both storms and success with remarkable discipline and restraint, a hallmark of this exceptional man.

Let us look at a few traits that have made Big B the living legend he is.

CLOCKWORK PUNCTUALITY

'Punctuality is the soul of business.'—THOMAS C. HALIBURTON

Among the popular stories in film circles about Amitabh Bachchan is his penchant for reaching the sets on time, if not with time to spare. It is said that his unfailing punctuality results in sleepless nights for his directors, who end up worrying about having to report on time themselves!

Bachchan's reputation for punctuality is almost as big as his superstardom and has truly withstood the test of time. For Express Adda, an informal chat session moderated by editor-in-chief of *Indian Express,* Shekhar Gupta, I had to escort the actor (from his Delhi residence) to the appointed venue. I reached well before the designated time, and was surprised to find him ready to leave. On being informed that we would probably arrive at the venue a little earlier than expected, he smiled, saying that he'd rather be early than late; he always preferred it that way. Through the course of the journey, the superstar was rather distressed about the traffic snarls en route. I realized that though he had factored in the travel time keeping in mind the distance, he had perhaps not bargained for the evening traffic in Delhi.

Despite minor delays, we reached ahead of time to find a thin crowd at the venue. I was embarrassed, assuming that he would be a tad disconcerted at the low turnout (a little later, the place was packed to capacity), but all I could see on his face was relief. He smiled reassuringly, and it suddenly dawned on me that the thought of people dropping in much later than him did not bother him as much as being late himself did.

I had met Bachchan on several occasions, but seeing this

legendary figure restless and worried about reaching on time for an event was a revelation to me. Especially since for chief guests, being late was par for the course. I realized that no matter what others expect of him, he goes to great lengths, factoring in every possible setback, ensuring that he is well in time for any event he attends.

Punctuality is not an ad hoc arrangement for Bachchan. It is a way of life, in his workspace, on social occasions or as a family man. It has helped create the rock-solid foundation he has based his life on.

At Express Adda, when asked about how he manages to pull off this punctuality, time and again, he laughed good-naturedly and replied, '*Ek yantra banaya gaya hai jise ghadi kehte hain. Main usey dekh kar samay se pahunch jaata hoon.* [There is an instrument called a watch. I look at it and reach on time.] There have been many times when I have arrived at the studio for a seven o' clock shift and nobody was there. So I utilized the time to water the plants and clean up the floor and things like that.'

If only it were that simple!

A punctual person effortlessly inspires confidence in others about his ability to get the job done. Unlike Bachchan, taking punctuality seriously and practising it with pride is something very few can claim to do. But as the saying goes, only a busy man can make time for everything.

UNWAVERING COMMITMENT

'Commitment is an act. Not a word.'—JEAN-PAUL SARTRE

It's absolutely true. Even after more than forty years as a leading actor with a zillion professional commitments, Bachchan remains true to his word. Put forward a proposal, and he is likely to give it due consideration before coming to a decision. Unlike several celebrities who consider it the norm to play the will-he-won't-he game, Big B is true to his word. As he asserted at Express Adda, 'I think you just need to honour a commitment if you have taken up a job.'

During the course of a personal conversation with me, Hema Malini, his co-star of many years, once said, 'Whether [sic] he was at the prime of his career, Amitabh is someone who has remained the same over time, a very remarkable quality in show business. He has always been polite and cooperative. If not keen to do something he would say so, explaining his reasons. None of that waiting-for-a-response ordeal with him.'

For *Screen*'s fifty-seventh anniversary party, I had put in a request for the superstar to be present as a guest of honour. After a few days, his office confirmed that he was willing and able to accept the invitation. Coincidentally, the event fell on the last day of Ganesh Chaturthi, a widely celebrated festival in Maharashtra, particularly Mumbai. By evening, the traffic around Marriott Hotel—the party venue—had turned absolutely chaotic. To make matters worse, it began pouring. I was fretting and anxious when his office called to say that he was on his way. Needless to say, we were jubilant at having the pleasure of Big B's company against all the odds! Even more impressive was the fact that after doing the honours, he took our leave and

> As an individual, I wish to be able to follow all the basic qualities that I was brought up with. Truth shall prevail, hard work shall be recognized, persistence in the right direction brings results, shortcuts in life have a short life.

left for yet another cultural function that he'd promised to be present at.

A person is as good as his word. Bachchan values this axiom and believes that he should accord the same respect to his word as he would want others to do to theirs. It is tough in the modern world to adhere to this seemingly old-fashioned value. Bachchan, who lives by this trait, is unstintingly appreciated by all.

WORK ETHICS

'Nothing will work unless you do.'—MAYA ANGELOU

That Amitabh Bachchan does not differentiate between big and small when it comes to his commitments is noteworthy. Once he has agreed to something, he treats a small function with the same respect he would accord a high-profile engagement. For instance, he is as diligent and excited when making a guest appearance in a film as he is when playing the lead. For the movie *Bol Bachchan* (2012), wherein he had a guest appearance in a song, he rehearsed his dance steps with the enthusiasm of a lead actor.

When shooting for *Paa* (2009), a home production made under the AB Corp. banner, Bachchan was required to wear elaborate prosthetics, as he was playing a progeria-afflicted child. He would spend hours putting on the elaborate make-up and endure the tedious wait without as much as a murmur.

A few years ago, he was to perform a short act at the Screen Awards to promote his film *Teen Patti* (2010). The act required him to sit on a throne-like chair and say a few lines, which he could have done in his sleep. Big stars are known to rehearse their steps for a show only at the last minute, but not Bachchan. He reported for rehearsals the night before the event and painstakingly went through the act, making sure that his co-actors were comfortable and had got their parts right too.

Perfection is achieved only when nothing is too small and every person in the team is considered equally important. It is only through the right combination of big and small tasks that one can achieve success. A committed person such as Bachchan is sincere towards the work he agrees to. He makes sure that even the smallest aspects of the task at hand are completed to his satisfaction.

> If I am healthy enough to breathe, I shall work. If there are people who wish to offer me a job, I shall consider it.

PROFESSIONALISM PERSONIFIED

'Being professional is just really clearly the way to go and helps you on the road to longevity.'—AMANDA SEYFRIED

According to colleagues, Bachchan never complains on the sets, no matter how inconvenient or uncomfortable the environs may be. Anupam Kher, his co-actor in many films, often relates an anecdote from the shooting of the film *Aakhree Raasta* (1986). The film was being shot in Chennai in sweltering heat and while everyone else was complaining about the air-conditioning, Bachchan, in his costume, complete with a shawl, was sitting quietly and reading. When asked how he could sit so calmly his answer was, 'If I don't think about the heat, I don't feel it.' This is perhaps the reason that Bachchan is accorded the status of a living legend.

Erstwhile leading actress Sadhana (of the Sadhana haircut fame), a close friend of the late producer Yash Johar, was once reminiscing about the days when Bachchan was working for him. Bachchan would be on the sets punctually, even though the director of the film would arrive late, at 11 a.m. A few other producers Bachchan was working with had located their sets close by, so that instead of wasting precious time, he sought permission from his producer (Johar) to work on these films till the director arrived. After pack up, he would head to yet another set, thus managing to pull off three shifts in a day.

He was credited with being a professional even at a time when stars were allowed the indulgence of reporting late on the sets, driving producers around the bend with their demands.

Rishi Kapoor, his colleague and family friend, has often said that Bachchan taught professionalism to the film industry. He never reported late, and he never had the entourage that accompanied other stars of the time.

Even today, after four decades in showbiz with all its accompanying crests and troughs, Bachchan's conduct is impeccable. After the glorious angry young man phase, the writ was that like his predecessors, his stardom too would fade imperceptibly. The critics could not have been more wrong. His legend has only grown because of his disciplined ways.

'As an individual, I wish to be able to follow all the basic qualities that I was brought up with. Truth shall prevail, hard work shall be recognized, persistence in the right direction brings results, shortcuts in life have a short life,' he reiterates, when asked about his impeccable work ethics.

Everybody appreciates a thorough professional, but there are few who maintain the strict boundaries necessary between work and personal life and consistently deliver a superlative performance. To sustain this for over four decades, while still maintaining the same level of exemplary professionalism, is a feat only the rarest of the rare can lay claim to. And Bachchan, with his unwavering discipline, deserves that honour.

CORRECT CONDUCT

'Propriety of manners and consideration for others are the two main characteristics of a gentleman.'—BENJAMIN DISRAELI

Among his other admirable virtues is the attention Bachchan pays to propriety. Be it a movie premiere, a meeting with an international celebrity, a prayer service for a departed colleague or simply a book launch, his conduct on all occasions is impeccable, his sentiments well-articulated with gracious words, his attire ever appropriate. On his seventieth birthday, Big B was at the entrance of a huge hall created in Mumbai's Film City studios, hands folded, welcoming everyone with a smile. He personally greeted all the guests (over a thousand), and was seen engaging everyone to join in the dancing and revelry.

'I feel like a citizen, whose every move is watched by the public, you need to behave yourselves and make sure you do not say the wrong things,' he once said.

An intrepid blogger, with fingerprints on Twitter and Facebook, Bachchan is extremely particular about updating his blog, even though it is not part of his professional duties. After an early blogging stint, he realized that his followers, whom he refers to as his 'extended family', eagerly await his daily updates; he now blogs diligently, frequently answering their queries.

In fact, on joining the micro-blogging site Twitter, he

punctiliously responded to every comment, resulting in his followers asking him to post fewer tweets as his replies were spamming their pages!

Whether learning about the newest social media additions or keeping in touch with his fans, Bachchan remains ahead because of his fastidious sense of duty. He delights in these tasks, making time even through punishing schedules—once, when I met him on the sets of *Paa*, he was readying for a quick blogging session during his lunch break!

> The media needs to designate me with something, like a superstar or legend, but for me, it is another day at work once I reach the set.

When in town on Sundays, he unfailingly steps out to wave to and greet the crowds outside his bungalow, a trend popular among his successors as well.

A man can be identified by his conduct. No matter what class or economic strata one belongs to, consideration in interaction defines a gentleman. Amitabh Bachchan continues to don the mantle effortlessly, yet again standing tall.

WORK IS WORSHIP

'Opportunity is missed by most people because it is dressed in overalls and looks like work.'—THOMAS ALVA EDISON

One of the most outstanding facets about the superstar was displayed when his company Amitabh Bachchan Corporation Limited (ABCL) was in the red. Instead of merely despairing, Bachchan went to director and long-standing friend Yash Chopra to ask him for work. It was his duty, he felt, to return the money that people had invested in his company. He was signed up for the film *Mohabbatein* (2000). Around the same time he took up *Kaun Banega Crorepati* or KBC (2000–), the Indian version of *Who Wants to be a Millionaire,* on the small screen. That was a time when no actor was willing to experiment with this medium. His dedication and charisma single-handedly turned *KBC* into an iconic show that is still synonymous with him.

Even at seventy-plus, Bachchan is willing to push the envelope. When he was shooting for the film *Satyagraha* (2013) in Bhopal, he abstained from regular meals in order to make his character, who was on a hunger strike, look authentic. And of course, it was business as usual when he braved the scorching heat with a black shawl for the said shoot while his junior colleagues rushed for cover.

Bachchan's leave of absence from work is minimal and usually restricted to doctors' edicts. 'If I am healthy enough to breathe, I shall work. If there are people who wish to offer me a job, I shall consider it.' Small wonder, then, that scores of people are still eager to work with Bachchan for as long as he is willing to do so.

Work is the only thing that sustains a person through his ups and downs. However, it is true that people get bogged down and disillusioned by the daily grind, only realizing its true worth when they don't have any job at hand. But in Amitabh Bachchan's case, work is worship at all times.

AGAINST ALL ODDS

'The bravest sight in the world is to see a great man struggling against adversity.'—LUCIUS ANNACUS SENECA

Among the various anecdotes Big B recalls is an incident from his childhood days that taught him an invaluable lesson for life. During his stint in Nainital's Sherwood School, he was preparing to participate in a school play when he fell ill and had to forego his role, making do with watching other children play their parts.

His father, Harivansh Rai Bachchan, who had gone to visit him, sensed his dismay and comforted him saying, '*Man ka ho to achcha, na ho to zyada achcha.*' (If things turn out the way you want, good, but if they don't, even better.)

Of course, it is not always easy to spot the silver lining, but even if a film fails to get the desired accolades, Bachchan continues putting in his best efforts, regardless of the results. After hosting the first two seasons of KBC, he remained unfazed when he was not reinstated as the host for Season 3 by the channel. He simply went on to anchor other television shows and act in notable films; lo and behold, his mass appeal and impeccable style had him return as *KBC*'s anchor in the next season. At last count, the show had completed seven seasons with Amitabh Bachchan as the host, a distinction no other superstar has enjoyed on television.

At Express Adda he made a very pertinent point about life's struggles. 'Somebody once asked me, "If you were to live your life again, what would you change?" I said that I wouldn't change anything because even the adversities taught me something. I would never have got these opportunities to learn [these] things had I not been through bad times. I would just let it remain as it is. Life for everybody is not going to be pleasant and it is not easy for everyone all the time. At times when I was very troubled, I used to go to my father and tell him, *"Babuji, sangharsh bada karna parta hai jeevan mein."* (Father, one has to struggle a lot in life.) He would say, *"Jab tak jeevan hai, tab tak sangharsh hai."* (While there is life, there is struggle.)'

In July 1982, Bachchan almost lost his life on the sets of *Coolie* (1983) during a fight sequence, when he fell from a blow delivered by co-actor Puneet Issar and ruptured his spleen. He was comatose and there was a brief moment in time when he was declared clinically dead. On the wings of prayers of his countless well-wishers, he survived to tell the tale. That battle between life and death is an example of his ability to persevere, to strive and battle against adversity. And yes, even death!

'We know that tomorrow you may be at a certain place and the day after things can go wrong. I think it is more important to realize how to fight it and move on, rather than dwell on what has happened in the past,' says Bachchan.

Despite myasthenia gravis and other health issues, even today he is steadfast in his determination to accomplish all the tasks that come his way. His blog entry, when he was requested by the mayor of London to run with the Olympic torch and flag off the London Olympics, is an example of that never-say-die attitude:

> Uniformed in the dress code of the Olympics and briefed on protocol and procedure, I am asked to cover a distance of 300 meters at South-wark [sic] in the Borough of London starting around 10:50 a.m.—a moment to be hopefully remembered by the

grandchildren. The run may not be possible keeping my surgery in mind, but there shall be effort made [sic] to move as close to it.

In the movies, it is only the hero of a story who can struggle against insurmountable odds and win in the end. Bachchan is a hero in real life, who faces every adversity that crosses his path with indomitable will.

THE DUTY OF HUMILITY

'Pride makes us artificial and humility makes us real.'
—THOMAS MERTON

Among other hallmark qualities that Big B has consistently maintained, one is humility. I recall my first encounter with him as a cub reporter on the sets of *Lal Badshah* (1999). I was quaking in my shoes at the prospect of meeting the biggest and most iconic star from Bollywood; imagine my surprise when he calmly extended his hand and said, 'I am Amitabh Bachchan, the actor!'

You could have knocked me down with a feather. Frankly speaking, I thought he had assumed me to be an idiot who knew nothing about movies, but it was actually his humility. Even today, when informed about any Hollywood star expressing his/her admiration for him, Bachchan is incredulous.

When Aamir Khan approached the superstar for a voiceover in *Lagaan* (2001) Bachchan agreed immediately. However, a few days later, director Ashutosh Gowariker changed his mind as he felt that the superstar's voice was too well-known to be effective for a period drama. Khan had to go back and inform

Bachchan of the same—a task he undertook most sheepishly. To his utter amazement, the superstar was gracious enough to not take umbrage, even admitting that he was vastly relieved, as some of the films that he had done voiceovers for had not fared very well. By a strange quirk of fate, it was eventually Bachchan's voice that narrated the story of *Lagaan*, the period drama that made box office history and went on to earn itself a nomination for the Oscars!

Big B's humility is as almost as legendary as his punctuality. He refuses to let praise go to his head, a big plus, especially for those working in the world of make-believe.

Of this ability to stay humble through his high-adrenaline life, he comments, 'As for the tags, they are like [government] designations in a government job—you become an officer, then secretary then joint secretary. The media needs to designate me with something, like a superstar or legend but for me, it is another day at work once I reach the set.'

Among his numerous qualities is a deep, abiding sense of duty, both personal and professional. The late film-maker Yash Chopra lauded him for being a model son, who lovingly cared for his ageing parents, tending to them through their twilight years with love and compassion. Even as a child, he was protective of his family. His brother Ajitabh Bachchan, on the occasion of his elder brother's seventieth birthday, recounted how Bachchan would shield him from the sun when they would cycle to school as young boys in Allahabad.

Always conscious of his responsibilities as a family man, Bachchan has often mentioned that his public conduct has been guided by two facts—that he is Harivansh Rai Bachchan's son as well as a father himself. 'As my father's son, I was born with this [celebrity-hood] so yes there were things that we were conscious of. Later on the responsibility became even more, twice as much...it was not only about being conscious of being my father's son, but also being father to my son.'

His interactions with fans and the extended family, the media and his work colleagues—mammoth tasks all—are governed by his unflinching sense of duty and humility.

Being humble is a value that is taught to all. But practising humility as a duty is the habit of just a few. The tendency to turn arrogant over one's achievements is hard to resist, but Bachchan leads by example—as a man who, even at the zenith of his superstardom, remains humble.

DISCIPLINE, BIG B STYLE

Discipline and duty are almost articles of faith for superstar Amitabh Bachchan, integral to everything he undertakes. They have played a significant role in his successful climb to the iconic stature he enjoys even today. In the showbiz top league his ability to be disciplined, professional and humble, besides his immense talent and an insatiable eagerness to work, immediately separate him from the crowd. Here's how discipline works in Big B's favour:

☆ **Dot on time:** Being punctual and courteous go a long way in making an impression. Everyone stands inarguably impressed and occasionally reformed when they have to contend with Bachchan's disciplined ways. It is one of the factors that lands him a dozen and more films, besides product endorsements and television projects, whose shooting schedules are far more punishing than film shoots.

☆ **Multitasking genius:** A by-product of punctuality is Bachchan's enviable multitasking ability. His discipline allows him to make room for multiple pursuits on several fronts, keeping him way ahead of his colleagues. He treats time with respect, using it for pursuits that are close to his heart and art. Spending time with family and friends, being part of television shows and commercials, fashion shoots, connecting with fans around the globe, meeting important dignitaries from the world of cinema—he juggles it all with enviable ease!

- ☆ **Family time:** In devoting time to the personal front along with the professional, Big B strikes that wonderful balance which those working in the corporate world try so hard to achieve. That he is a family man, who considers time with wife, children and grandchildren as important as his professional chores, increases people's awe and admiration for him. When relationships are maintained with family and friends, the support system, especially in a demanding profession, is tremendous.
- ☆ **Humble approach:** For a career based on popularity, as acting is, humility is very effective in making it last. At seventy-plus, Bachchan's career is still going strong, testimony to how well humility has worked for him.

SHAH RUKH KHAN

Passion

'Better pass boldly into that other world,
in the full glory of some passion, than fade and
wither dismally with age.'

—JAMES JOYCE

'At that moment I knew I could fly'—that was Shah Rukh Khan, explaining his cartwheels and attempt to fly around the stadium after his Indian Premier League (IPL) victory in 2012. And somehow it sounded believable. Given the superstar's success story—a middle-class young man who came to Mumbai with a dream and turned himself into Hindi cinema's biggest superstar—it is easy to believe that he can make the unimaginable happen. Khan's is a true modern-day fairy tale, one that he has authored with infinite passion.

He often remarks, 'I truly believe that I cannot fail. I came to Mumbai with ₹1,500 and I know I will have ₹1,500 even when I leave, so how can I be a failure?'

Let's go back in time to trace Khan's entry into films—the starting point of his showbiz career was playing Abhimanyu Rai in the television series *Fauji* (1988). The series gained huge popularity and he featured in yet another TV show, *Dil Dariya* (1988–1989). The recognition and appeal of the shows landed him a couple of film offers but Khan was happy working in television and theatre in Delhi. However, fate had other plans. A two-part episode in *Ummeed* (1989), a serial that was being produced by directors Aziz Mirza, Saeed Mirza and Kundan Shah, brought him to Mumbai. Soon after, he was signed on for the serial *Circus* (1989–1990). His stint in Mumbai gave him exposure to a different work culture, one that was far more professional and bigger in scale. Once again, film offers began coming his way and he made tracks towards Bollywood. Fortunately, he had struck a great rapport with Aziz and Saeed Mirza, who had hosted him during his early years in Mumbai, sparing him the much-romanticized filmy struggle of sleeping on pavements or railway stations.

Khan's first role was in Hema Malini's *Dil Aashna Hai*

(1992) followed by *Deewana* (1992). And there's been no looking back since.

Today, Khan remains the biggest superstar in Bollywood with scores of awards (including Screen Awards) and honours conferred on him in India, France, Egypt and Malaysia for his work in cinema, including the Padma Shri. He's also the proud co-owner of Kolkata Knight Riders (KKR), an IPL cricket team; KidZania, a children's edutainment park; and owner of Red Chillies Entertainment, a production house that has its fingers in several pies—films, special-effects facilities, film-making equipment, television production and live events.

'My wife tells me I work too much. Actually, I like working. I like ideas, but right now I would like to devote time to my children. They are growing up and I want to be there [for them] during that period,' says the superstar.

Here are a few traits that have propelled Shah Rukh Khan to the enviable position he is in today.

In India, for some of my earlier films I have said '*Yeh achcha nahin lag raha hai*' (This is not looking nice), and the response has been, '*Theek hai yaar! Koi fark nahin padta hai*' (It's okay. It doesn't make a difference). It is the biggest destructive line. Unless we push the bar in terms of standards, we will always be substandard in comparison to the world. What would be really fantastic is to use world-class technology to make a film for the Indian market. For people to watch it and say, 'Wow! World standard hai!'

CONFIDENCE 24X7

'With confidence, you have won even before you have started.'
—MARCUS GARVEY

Ask anyone who met Khan at the outset of his career and they will tell you about his overwhelming confidence. 'I will be a superstar,' is what he told everyone. At that time, it seemed implausible, if not foolish, bragging to some, but he made good his promise. It is a story that has long passed into Bollywood folklore, continuing to inspire younger generations that come into the film industry. The 'Yes, I can!' attitude is one of the most impressive things about Khan, a confidence both winning and inspiring.

According to the superstar, his father Mir Taj Mohammed Khan made everything in life seem like fun, a reason he enjoys work immensely. His father also taught him to be responsible for his actions at a very young age. In his biography (on www.iamshahrukhkhan.com), Khan mentions an incident that is insightful—at the age of four, he beat up one of the boys in his neighbourhood and injured him. When the boy's father took Khan to task, threatening to kill him for hurting his son, Khan's father sent him out to make his own excuses for hurting the boy! In his recollection of the story, the superstar admits that he was scared at being left to stand up for himself. He apologized profusely to the father of the injured boy and peace prevailed, but his dad's message stayed with him—he would have to clean up his own mess. This invaluable lesson, among other things, has certainly held him in good stead, for the superstar always takes responsibility for his actions, is unafraid to speak his mind and has the courage and confidence to reach out for the seemingly impossible.

To shoulder one's responsibility with aplomb and look every difficulty squarely in the eye is the mark of a man destined for success. In Khan's case, his confidence is often mistaken for brashness, but when one interacts with him, one realizes that it is not arrogance but just the strength of his convictions, a clearly spelt out statement of intent, which helps him steer ahead.

KINDNESS

'A little thought and a little kindness are often worth more than a great deal of money.'—JOHN RUSKIN

Khan has the unique ability to be attentive to everyone around him. More significantly, despite his superstar status, he doesn't talk down to people. Even at press conferences teeming with hundreds of media persons, he can establish a connection with pretty much everyone in the room.

At a promotional event for his film *My Name Is Khan* (2010), a young scribe mispronounced a particular name and had the crowd tittering at the faux pas. Khan, on the other hand, to put the journalist at ease, cracked a joke with flourish and repeated the entire sentence verbatim, reading out the mispronounced word correctly for the benefit of the youngster. It was a small gesture, but immeasurable in its empathy.

Another instance that comes to mind was while he was hosting the television show *Kya Aap Paanchvi Paas Se Tez Hain?* (2008) on Star Plus, which tested the knowledge of its adult participants against that of fifth-grade students. The show had opened to a mixed response, but it had, among others, found an ardent admirer in my grandmother, who liked it for its knowledge quotient. She asked me to pass on her compliments to Khan, which I did.

He immediately responded with a text message that said, 'Please thank your grandma and give her my love. Inshallah, I may be back with another season.' Grandma was delighted beyond measure!

Such anecdotes of Khan's kindness abound. While shooting a crucial sequence for *Don 2* (2011) on an outdoor location in Berlin, the temperature suddenly plummeted; Khan called for a break immediately, turning his attention to the comfort of the crew, checking whether they were warm and well looked after.

Yet another anecdote involves actor–producer Vivek Vaswani, who was instrumental in Khan getting some of his initial roles in films. Many years later, when Vaswani was struggling to produce a film (*Dulha Mil Gaya*, 2010) he asked Khan to do a special appearance in it. Without even looking at the script or hearing the story, Khan agreed. In a cut-throat world, his kindness and inclusiveness make him extremely popular with people across the spectrum. His ability to put people at ease and encourage them is an invaluable boon. After all, films change every Friday, while an act of kindness stays with a person for life.

It is the little things we do that make a big difference in how people perceive us. A great man is one who cares for the smallest member of his team. Khan considers this practice sacrosanct. His small gestures make his persona larger than life.

BE THE BEST

'Doing the best at this moment puts you in the best place for the next moment.'—OPRAH WINFREY

Khan's famous claim 'I am the best' has often met with mixed reactions.

Some people think it is arrogance, but making an effort to be the best in every endeavour he takes on is continuous and constant in his case. He is driven to always be the best. As he has mentioned in press interviews, he wants everyone to do well, but he just wants to do better than the rest!

Be it acting or life, if there is one thing that Khan has an aversion to, it is the 'chalta hai' attitude.

A small example of his emphasis on excellence is his preoccupation with special effects and animation (recent additions to Indian cinema). Over the years, besides being a leading star, Khan has created Red Chillies Entertainment, his own film-making company, which, in addition to producing films, covers all technical aspects of cinema, including special effects. He tried to push the envelope in this regard with his mega home production *Ra.One* (2011), a superhero film for which a lot of the special work was done at his homegrown Red Chillies' special effects (VFX) facility. They also did some superlative work in *Krrish 3* (2013), again a hit superhero film.

In *Ra.One*, Khan gave us perhaps for the first time an Indian superhero with a definitive costume, besides a film with world-class special effects. There is a breathtaking scene where a speeding train breaks out of the Chhatrapati Shivaji Terminus and lands on the road, all achieved by visual-effect teams within India. The quality vies with the best in the world because Khan would not settle for anything less from his own company.

'In India, for some of my earlier films I have said *"Yeh achcha nahin lag raha hai"* (This is not looking nice), and the response has been, *"Theek hai yaar! Koi fark nahin padta hai"* (It's okay. It doesn't make a difference). It is the biggest destructive line. Unless we push the bar in terms of standards, we will always be substandard in comparison to the world. What would be really fantastic is to use world-class technology to make a film for the Indian market. For people to watch it and say, "Wow! World standard hai!"' Khan once said.

Only those who shrug aside their limitations and put in their best emerge winners, as Khan has proven time and again. His eagerness to do a job to the best of his ability or make the most of a situation is worth emulating. After all, one's circumstances are not always under one's control, but one's actions are.

MONEY: MEANS TO AN END

'A wise man should have money in his head, but not in his heart.'—JONATHAN SWIFT

Just a short while before he passed away, veteran director Yash Chopra, during a live chat session with Khan, mentioned that among other things, the reason he chose the superstar over others to act in all his recent films was because, 'He never asks me how much money I will be paying him or what his role is. He just wants me to tell him when we are going to start shooting.'

Yash Chopra's endorsement of Khan's passion for cinema reiterates the claim the actor has often made—he does not act in movies for money. During the making of *Ra.One*, although he had a studio on board to finance the project, he roped in all the brands he endorses for funding the film. This was done to ease the financial burden without compromising on the visual quality, so crucial for the perfect superhero film.

'We should use the money that we are getting to make better films. Not to take it back home. Make a spectacular film and the money will follow. I made no money from *Deewana*, I made no money from *Raju Ban Gaya Gentleman* [1992] and very little money from *Baazigar* [1993] or *Dilwale Dulhaniya Le Jayenge* [1995] compared to what one asks for now. But the films made me the star that I am. We get so absorbed in this race for money that we forget the core,' believes Khan.

But he has a healthy respect for money and what it can achieve. However, he sees it more as a means to achieve an end—a comfortable life—and for increasing his avenues as an entertainer. The income generated from endorsements, live performances, etc. are ploughed back into his companies that produce entertainment software—movies, television shows, IPL and more.

According to Khan, 'I love being rich. I never have any qualms in telling people that you should be well-to-do according to your own standards. Whatever makes you happy. I

I'd rather fail creating something new than keep doing the same thing even though I am the one star who is blamed for doing the same thing all the time. I do try to push the envelope in my own way and I put my money where my mouth is because I owe it to myself and my audience.

---

am a house person and I like my house and I am happy with it. I have no extravagant habits except movies. My favourite waste of money is making films. I don't waste money on anything else.'

Money is a by-product of one's passion. Khan's aim is not to sit and watch his money grow—he believes, instead, in using the money to fuel his passion for cinema by making the kind of movies he wants, with adequate technology to support it.

NEVER GIVE UP

'I am not discouraged because every wrong attempt discarded is a step forward.'—THOMAS ALVA EDISON

During the making of *Ra.One*, there was a scene in which Khan was required to do a quick somersault from a motorbike and land on his feet. As is common practice, there was a stuntman at hand to do the needful, but Khan insisted on performing the stunt himself, even though he had been suffering from a knee injury. He repeated his moves till director Anubhav Sinha had his perfect shot. Just another example of his never-say-die spirit.

About a decade ago, in 2000, when Khan was at the peak of his career, he was widely hailed by the media as 'badshah' and 'king'. Then the winds of change blew, and it looked as though Bollywood was going to see a change in regime. Hrithik Roshan had taken everyone by surprise with a dazzling debut in *Kaho Naa...Pyaar Hai* (2000). It did not help that Khan's home production *Phir Bhi Dil Hai Hindustani,* which released just a week later, failed to make an impression. Comparisons were unavoidable. That a newcomer's film had gathered more footfalls than the superstar's had trade pundits in the media jump the gun to declare the end of Khan's glorious innings as the Numero Uno.

Though upset by the criticism, Khan took it stoically and went on to prove everyone wrong. He even shared screen space with Roshan in *Kabhi Khushi Kabhie Gham* (2001). They have been friends ever since. More recently, one witnessed his resilience when his film *Chennai Express* (2013) raked in over ₹200 crore in India (and around 19.5 million USD worldwide) beating his contemporaries' box office records of ₹100 crore. This, in an extremely competitive scenario packed with scores of talented newcomers and peers. The significant point here is that Khan did not give up on his dream even under the most trying circumstances.

Another instance of his never-say-die spirit was evident in the way he handled his IPL team, KKR. During the first four IPL seasons, their performance was unimpressive, with the team struggling to find its rhythm. Khan, though disappointed, did not lose heart. He worked closely with the team manager and the players to help turn the tide. After several rounds of rethinking, and taking the risky decision of replacing captain Sourav Ganguly (Kolkata's blue-eyed boy), along with some smart strategizing, in 2012, KKR beat the reigning champions Chennai Super Kings (CSK) by five wickets in a high-scoring final!

Failure, as Khan has always maintained, is not discouraging for him. 'I'd rather fail creating something new than keep doing the same thing even though I am the one star who is blamed for doing the same thing all the time. I do try to push the envelope in my own way and I put my money where my mouth is because I owe it to myself and my audience.

'I have grown up watching Amitji [Amitabh Bachchan]

and yes, there have been times when he is hurt, or angry and disturbed with the world not because people have let him down but because he feels he did not try hard enough. This desire to prove yourself good enough again and again for the audience which has made you, without being cynical is what makes you a legend.'

Like the proverbial spider in the King Bruce story, it is important to not give up. Especially when all looks lost. Failure may dog your footsteps, but success eventually comes if you don't stop trying. Khan has experienced glorious success and bitter failures, and yet he has never turned his back on the job at hand. It is for this reason that despite newer stars on the horizon, he continues to shine brightly as ever.

THINK BIG

'Ordinary people believe only in the possible. Extraordinary people visualise not what is possible or probable, but rather what is impossible. And by visualising the impossible, they begin to see it as possible.'—CHERIE CARTER-SCOTT

While a lot of people think him to be a shrewd businessman, passion is what drives Khan in all his endeavours. He often says, 'I can't be part of a small project. Once I am a part of it, it no longer remains small!'

Now, a declaration of that kind may smack of narcissism but in the superstar's case, it is a simple statement of fact. Each time he takes up a project he tries to make it the best, bringing in the latest technology, talent, practically everything within his power to make it a fine piece of work. He spent generously on all aspects of *Ra.One*, including the superhero suit, the most innovative so far in Indian films. He roped in international pop singer Akon to sing the song 'Chammak Challo' for the film and probably would have signed up Hollywood star Gerard Butler for the antagonist's role, except that the script required an oriental villain.

At a time when featuring in ads was frowned upon by actors, Khan signed up for a handful, using these earnings to start his own production company to make the kind of movies that he liked. This was the genesis of Dreamz Unlimited, in collaboration with actor Juhi Chawla and Aziz Mirza. He started off with *Phir Bhi Dil Hai Hindustani*, a satire on the commercialization of media (made in the mainstream Hindi film format). Despite the risky subject, the superstar refused to cut corners. His next film, *Asoka* (2001), an epic on the life of Emperor Ashoka, was equally audacious. The company has since given way to his production house Red Chillies Entertainment, which has several hits, including *Chennai Express*, to its credit.

> Passion is a pre-requisite for success. I think I am passionate in that when I do something, I like to do it to the best of my ability. So I get very excited by what I am doing at the moment and when I am out of that, I get excited about the next thing.

Big people think big. They have the ability to spot the extraordinary in what seems mundane to others. Khan's ability to look beyond the obvious and turn every small opportunity into a big deal is the hallmark of a great mind, the reason why he is considered an icon.

HAVE A LAUGH

'Common sense and a sense of humor are the same thing, moving at different speeds. A sense of humor is just common sense, dancing.'—WILLIAM JAMES

'My father told me to be honest, hard-working and have a sense of humour,' says Khan, known for his razor-sharp and wry wit. While it may land him in trouble with co-stars, it certainly makes him the media's blue-eyed boy. It is not just that he is witty but his humour is laced with impressive intelligence. His liveliness and presence of mind has saved many a function or press conference from turning into a drab and dull event.

It is a fact that all Khan press conferences are high wattage and well attended because of his ability to be light-hearted. On his part, he always maintains that his wife has forbidden him from cracking too many jokes, as it often gets him into trouble! However, that does not stop him from poking fun at himself. Sample this: 'In Europe, they may not recognize me, but they know who Shah Rukh Khan is.'

At another public event, he jested about *Ra.One*, a film he was producing and acting in at the time. 'In the film industry when someone tells you that your film is "ahead of its time" that means the film will not work. I hope *Ra.One* is not ahead of times. If it is, I will go back in time working like the labour class doing all kinds of television shows and films.'

To possess a sense of humour, and to be able to laugh at oneself does not come easy. Most of us take ourselves too seriously; we would rather that the joke be on someone else! But be it a sticky situation or an awkward one, wit always comes in handy as it does with Khan. His quick-witted comments, especially those directed at himself, keep everyone amused, making him even more endearing to his colleagues and admirers.

PASSION PLAY

'Passion rebuilds the world for the youth. It makes all things alive and significant.'—RALPH WALDO EMERSON

From the outset, Khan has been synonymous with the passion that he brings to the table. Co-star Kareena Kapoor says that Khan is 200 per cent dedication, with energy reserves that most of us can just dream of. Whether it is a routine press interview, a lecture at Harvard University or hosting an award show function, he is passionately involved, infusing boundless energy into everything.

When he was the guest for Express Adda at the Olive restaurant, Mumbai, he stayed for over two and a half hours instead of the designated hour and a half, chatting with people on a variety of subjects, from cricket to personal relationships. He even recited a few lines of Urdu shayari and broke into the famous 'Chammak Challo' steps from his film *Ra.One* in between. No wonder he had everybody eating out of his hands.

More recently, when Khan's team was shooting for *Happy New Year* (forthcoming[*]) in Dubai, the star not only completed his shooting commitments and put in an appearance at the press conference organized by the local authorities, he even hosted a party afterwards at his Palm Jumaeirah residence

---
[*]At the time of writing

for the entire team. He chatted amicably, boosting their morale and sharing work tips till the wee hours of the morning.

About his boundless enthusiasm, Khan says, 'Passion is a pre-requisite for success. I think I am passionate in that when I do something, I like to do it to the best of my ability. So I get very excited by what I am doing at the moment and when I am out of that, I get excited about the next thing.'

Being charged up about what one is doing is half the battle won. Without passion, even the most interesting job can seem dreary. Khan on the other hand, excels in the art of making even drab, regular activities fun, both for himself and everyone else involved in it. His unmatchable passion, stemming from a genuine interest in the task at hand, gives him an edge over others.

THE CASE OF A CURIOUS MIND

'The important thing is not to stop questioning. Curiosity has its own reason for existing.'—ALBERT EINSTEIN

The bandwidth of subjects that interest Khan is fairly wide, ranging from books, cinema, sports and politics to gadgets. Once, he asked a group of people the meaning of the word 'lenticular'. No one knew the answer, but Khan did not rest till he discovered that it was a particular technology used in film posters.

He encourages people to ask questions, though not meaningless ones. 'I don't answer to stupidity,' he says, but on a good day, he is the only superstar who does not take a 'No comments' stance!

This natural curiosity has helped Khan stay ahead of the

competition, making him a crowd favourite. Given his brilliant mind, it is hardly surprising that he can engage and entertain with ease; in fact, surveys have bestowed the tag of a 'modern legend' upon him. The superstar's reaction to this news was characteristically earnest, yet irreverent.

'I have always believed I am going to be real in real life. It's not special to be special. It's special to be ordinary even though you are a big movie star. I have six guards and big cars and a big house but my car is not an extension of my personality. These are all accessories that I have accumulated along the way and they make life very comfortable, very nice. But if I did not have the six bodyguards, or the car or the house, it would still not be very different. I will have the same strengths and weaknesses; and I would still like to read books.'

Constant learning is such an undervalued quality. Only the brightest minds continue to feed their curiosity. The easiest way to reach stagnation is to declare oneself an expert. Khan's keenness to always keep abreast with trends and developments in all fields takes him way ahead of his peers. Being widely informed on a variety of subjects enables him to become part of several pursuits in addition to movies, granting him an iconic status.

BEING THE BEST,
THE SHAH RUKH KHAN WAY

As Khan says, 'My audience is my employer and I am glad they think I am doing a good enough job. I hope I will not be removed from my job anytime soon.'

In a bid to keep the dream job forever, Khan ensures that there is no dull moment in his life or, for that matter, his audience's. The remarkable part is that each endeavour is undertaken and dealt with equal passion. As he famously says, he would rather burn out than rust away.

A crash course in making it to the top league and staying there, King Khan style:

☆ **Make each moment count:** The most enviable quality of Shah Rukh Khan is the matchless enthusiasm (co-stars describe it as his infectious energy) that he displays for each and every second of work at hand. It may be an ad shoot, an interview or a film; Khan puts in 200 per cent, as though it were the most important thing in the world for him. His enthusiasm is not linked to the money he is being paid. Press conferences held for even the most mundane announcements, such as the launch of a new credit card or financial service, turn entertaining if Khan is the star guest, making him an instant hit. When he is on board for a project, he ensures that his investors get their money's worth. If it is an award function he is hosting, he will deliver the goods with aplomb—play the perfect host, walk the red carpet and sit in the audience without any fuss. His wit and charm, of course, make him delightful and sought-after company, which is a huge plus in a business where stars are better known for their tantrums and long list of demands.

★ **Goodness gracious:** Khan's ability to see the good in situations is what makes him a winner, time and again. Like the childhood incident when his father ensured that he took responsibility for his actions, and the boy realized that his father's leaving him in the cold was a bid to make him responsible. Though he may tell you that he does not like criticism, Khan is that rare person who accepts contrarian views and even jests about it in a characteristic self-deprecating manner. Coupled with his magnanimity towards co-stars, colleagues and pretty much everyone he interacts with, his ability to focus on positivity and never give up makes him a winner, a real-life hero, emulated by millions around the world.

★ **Wealth of knowledge:** Khan has a wide range of interests and a natural curiosity for all kinds of information. He is as aware and informed about cricket as he is about the media business, photography or management principles. Extremely fond of reading, he enjoys science fiction, crime thrillers and classics—not necessarily in that order (Douglas Adams is among his favourite authors). This, coupled with his natural charm and sense of humour, helps him hold forth on any topic easily. Whether addressing business school graduates, the Indian cricket team, the Bollywood brigade or corporate czars, Shah Rukh Khan is enthusiastically up to it. It's actually an interesting synergy—his deep interest and knowledge in various subjects help him expand laterally by connecting with people in different walks of life. He is invited to speak at leadership summits and Ivy League universities such as Harvard and, yes, nobody goes away disappointed.

☆ **Money well spent:** There's nothing that excites Khan as much as a good idea or a worthy challenge. Money, therefore, is a medium to follow his dreams with passion. Although he's been severely criticized for dancing at weddings and taking up too many endorsements, he uses these earnings primarily for his movies. He has always maintained that his businesses will be related to entertainment—the IPL team, VFX facilities and film equipment, Kidzania Edutainment Park and a cricket academy. Though a top star, his professional fee is always reasonable. With a clear understanding that business should not be run with personal money, or by mortgaging houses—as was the norm in the Bollywood of yore—Khan has followed a business model that generates enough revenues to support and sustain itself. The important thing is that money, for him, is a means to achieve his goals—make better films and create facilities that help improve the standard of film-making. He does not aspire to become the richest man in the world.

VIDYA BALAN

Reinvention

'You have to reinvent yourself every day, and that means being a pioneer.'

—FREDERIC DE NARP, PRESIDENT AND CEO, CARTIER

That Vidya Balan is an excellent actress, the quintessential desi girl, and an extremely proud one at that, is well known. But the National Award winner (who bagged all the film awards for four consecutive years) stands out for several other reasons. Her choice of roles, for starters, has been a trailblazer. By picking movies that establish actresses as equals to their male counterparts, Balan has single-handedly empowered the Hindi film heroine.

Blessed with traditional good looks, she has reinstated the Indian heroine to a proud position and while at it, has turned the humble nine-yard handspun sari into a renewed style statement.

After four successful heroine-dominated films—*Ishqiya* (2010), *No One Killed Jessica* (2011), *The Dirty Picture* (2011) and *Kahaani* (2012)—Balan received the ultimate praise reserved for a heroine—the sobriquet of the fourth Khan (joining the ranks of Bollywood's leading trio, Aamir, Salman and Shah Rukh)! In the testosterone-driven world of the Bollywood box office, to be considered a male star's equivalent in making a film successful is a significant achievement.

In a span of seven years, Balan's courageous reinvention of the heroine's role in mainstream cinema has earned her a legion of fans around the world—so much so that she was even invited to be a part of the prestigious jury for the 66th Festival de Cannes, headed by the renowned film-maker Steven Spielberg.

For Balan, who has followed film actors since she was a teenager (she practised crying naturally in front of the mirror, because she had heard that Shabana Azmi did not use glycerine while shedding tears on-screen), life has indeed shaped up Cinderella-like, complete with a Prince Charming.

Glory and honour notwithstanding, Vidya Balan's journey

has been a tough one. She had to fight several battles before being declared the winner and to her credit, she did not let go of her dream to be an actor. From being considered too traditional, plain and even unlucky before being lauded as a game-changer on her own terms, Balan cuts an inspiring figure.

Though her career is currently a work-in-progress, there are certainly a few things one can learn from the Bebaak (uninhibited) Balan on how to get your mojo back and make it shine anew.

> The moment I liberated myself from the pressure of fitting in, the scripts just started pouring in. *Paa* happened, then *Ishqiya*, *The Dirty Picture*, *No One Killed Jessica* and *Kahaani* happened. I just needed to free myself.

DEAL WITH FAILURE

'I can accept failure, everyone fails at something. But I can't accept not trying.'—MICHAEL JORDAN

When Balan's debut film *Parineeta* (2005) was about to hit the marquee, word was that though the new girl from Chembur (a Mumbai suburb) showed promise, she was an unconventional choice to be cast opposite heavy-hitters Saif Ali Khan and Sanjay Dutt. After all she was twenty-five, way too old to embark on an acting career. It was not known then that Balan was destined to turn convention on its head, time and again.

Though she did have some acting experience (she played one of five sisters in Ekta Kapoor's TV comedy *Hum Paanch* [1995–2006]), her film stint, so far, had been unremarkable.

Balan had run into rough weather when trying her hand at Malayalam films—she was dropped from about twelve, along with two Tamil films, because producers dubbed her 'unlucky'. It was a very difficult time for her and her parents, but the spunky girl had set her heart on an acting career. Despite the rejections, she was firm about not giving up just because she couldn't make it in the South.

Balan had something that could appeal to another set of film-makers. She looked to the east and found a foothold in Bengali films, besides pitching for TV commercials and a few music videos (for the band Euphoria). She managed to feature in several of the latter as the lead model. It was while shooting for TV ads that she met director Pradeep Sarkar, who cast her in his advertisements before launching her career in Hindi movies with *Parineeta*.

The producer of the film, Vidhu Vinod Chopra, had been keen to cast Aishwarya Rai Bachchan for the role but Sarkar insisted on his original choice, Vidya Balan. She had to undergo several rounds of auditions, but since she was already conversant with the Bengali ethos, she came across as a natural, eventually receiving Chopra's nod. *Parineeta* was a huge success and Balan's traditional beauty, grace and acting prowess had the critics' as well as the industry veterans' unanimous approval.

Speaking of her failures, Balan admits that she was shaken but kept the faith. She was brave enough to even reject a television serial offered to her by director Anurag Basu while she was in talks for *Parineeta*. Had she given up acting after her initial failure down South, the world would have never experienced her immense talent. Instead, she analysed her ambition candidly. 'I was born to act,' she avers. And so, when one door closed, she purposefully knocked on another, disregarding the daunting possibility of failure. In the process, she learnt never to give up and the rest, as they say, is history.

TRADITIONAL IS BEAUTIFUL

'I am a woman in process. I'm just trying like everybody else. I try to take every conflict, every experience, and learn from it. Life is never dull.'—OPRAH WINFREY

Balan, in the early flush of success, was just settling down to her new job of a full-fledged Bollywood heroine when the tide turned once again. The heady success of *Parineeta* and *Lage Raho Munna Bhai* (2006) was followed by severe criticism of her nondescript roles in *Heyy Babyy* (2007) and *Kismat Konnection* (2008). Adding to her misery was the constant hounding by the fashion police. Their verdict was clear—she did not know her Prada from her Gucci and was certainly not the perfect clothes horse! In blindly following others, one tends to ignore or undermine the unique qualities one possesses. The tirade propelled her from one fashion faux pas to another. Her clothes, her accessories, her hairstyle—all were under fire. From being the girl who could do no wrong, she was reduced to a fashion wreck.

There was a certain cockiness on my part—I thought that those roles required me to sleepwalk through them because I had the appreciation as an actor. I was sadly mistaken because everything you do on screen, even sleeping on the screen, has to be done convincingly. You can't do it, thinking—*Arrey, kisiko kya pata chalega?*

At a time when size zero ruled supreme, Balan with her 'Indian' frame stood out for her curvaceous figure. Though apologetic in the beginning for her traditional style, the actress turned the tables on her critics and fans alike with her volte-face from wannabe-skinny to proud-to-be-curvy. During the shooting of *Paa* at Whistling Woods in Film City, it was a pleasant surprise to observe someone not insisting on green tea or health bars and salad bowls, but enjoying regular Indian khana. A few years later, she was brave enough to gain weight for her role in *The Dirty Picture* before gamely adding on a few more pounds to play a 'hatti-katti' Punjabi woman in *Ghanchakkar* (2013)!

At a promotional event for the film *Ferrari Ki Sawaari* (2012), in which Balan danced to a Lavani number, the actress, who had piled on the kilos, managed to pull off the sexy moves with such aplomb that the audience just couldn't get enough of her! Her confidence and joie de vivre more than compensated for the lack of skinny stats and washboard abs.

'I came into the industry not as a girl, but as a woman, both in terms of age and the character that I was playing. Again, it is very liberating to realize that how you feel about yourself has very little to do with your body shape. *The Dirty Picture* helped me figure that out. I am a certain body type and will never be skinny and I am fine with that. As an actor, I have to enjoy being in my own skin when I am not in someone else's. I do hope women become more accepting of their bodies because a large part of our self-esteem derives from the perception of our bodies,' sums up the actor.

With this statement, she turned what others perceived as a shortcoming into a formidable strength. And in doing so, Balan became a pioneer of sorts.

FOLLOW YOUR HEART, NOT STEREOTYPES

'Don't follow a trend. Follow your heart.'—Krist Novoselic

After the initial euphoria and subsequent despair (of not getting the right roles) had run its course, the actress took a brave leap of faith when she agreed to play mother to then sixty-seven-year-old Amitabh Bachchan in the film *Paa*! Sceptics rushed to write an epitaph to her fledgling career. There were sarcastic whispers about Balan being the new Nirupa Roy on the block (Roy had played Bachchan's mother in several films in the 1970s).

As it turned out, the film and the three central characters, played by Amitabh Bachchan, Abhishek Bachchan and Vidya Balan, were heaped with praise; Balan even went on to win a series of awards for her bravura performance as a young single mother to a thirteen-year-old born with progeria—a disease that causes premature ageing and death. Once again, by sticking to her guns, she took a huge risk and turned it into a success. She swept all the film awards that year.

Post *Paa*, just when one imagined that she would now be landing similar 'mother' roles, she surprised everyone as the foxy Krishna from a small village in Uttar

> So, that's the biggest lesson I learnt when I went through all that criticism for doing indifferent work. There was criticism about the clothes; there was criticism about *Heyy Babyy*, criticism on pretty much everything. At that time it is difficult to digest. In trying to fit in and not making any effort in the right direction, I was sticking out like a sore thumb.

Pradesh in *Ishqiya*, who uses her sexuality as a tool for survival. Till this point, Balan with her girl-next-door charm had never been considered sexy. She took up the challenge and turned the character into a saucy widow who employs sex for her physical needs as well as to meet other ends. Balan's ability to pull of the steamy scenes with conviction impressed even the toughest critics on the block.

Then came *The Dirty Picture,* which saw Balan propel this new, improved version of herself to dizzying heights.

Reminiscing about the earlier phase of following prevalent trends, she says, 'I did go through that wanting-to-adhere-to-norm, because I was being appreciated.

'*Parineeta* was like living a dream. Then [*Lage Raho*] *Munna Bhai* happened and it was a huge success. No one criticized me. Yet, there was nothing defining as an actor except that my signature call from the film, "Good morning, Mumbai", captured everybody's imagination. It was not earth-shattering perhaps, but I went along, feeling that maybe it was because I was still not playing the stereotypical heroine. *Heyy Babyy* and *Kismat Konnection* were two films in which I did that. I wanted to do those typical roles. There was nothing wrong with those films—it was "I" in those films.

'One day, at a nail parlour, a lady walked up to me and said, "There's only one of you so why are you trying to be someone else?" Of course, at that time it was difficult to digest it,' recalls the actor.

But the thought took root, prompting her to take the next steps without fear, because in her heart she had always known that she was made to break new ground. In her words, 'The moment I liberated myself from the pressure of fitting in, the scripts just started pouring in. *Paa* happened, then *Ishqiya, The*

Dirty Picture, No One Killed Jessica and *Kahaani* happened. I just needed to free myself.'

Following stereotypes is easy. But people like Balan break moulds and earn admiration, because walking in a new direction requires courage.

THE METHOD IN MADNESS

'Strength does not come from winning. Your struggles develop your strengths. When you go through hardships and decide not to surrender, that is strength.'—ARNOLD SCHWARZENEGGER

The script and her role in the film is something that Balan is particular about, especially after the debacles her career has witnessed. 'It's nice to do different things and to know what you want to do and what you don't. At one time I wanted to do purely commercial cinema and the films met the criteria. After *Heyy Babyy* and *Kismat Konnection*, a lot of people told me that I was wasted in the films; I needed to do roles that were more fleshed out. When the challenge is greater, I am able to give it my best.'

Her mentor Pradeep Sarkar says that Balan has always had a 'keeda'—a hunger—for good roles, for pushing the limits. She is an actor who likes to prepare, read the script before the shoot and, by her own admission, ask a lot of questions. 'I would say that I prefer myself in *Kismat Konnection* to *Heyy Babyy*. They are two films I hadn't read the script [of] before I went to shoot. For *Kismat Konnection*, I had thought of reading the script once I reached Canada but I couldn't. I went to sleep and woke up the next morning just in time for the shoot! I panicked and started crying,' she recalls. 'It was almost a forewarning.'

Having learnt the pitfalls of sleepwalking through films, the actress subsequently worked very hard in getting the nuances right for her part. 'There was a certain cockiness on my part—I thought that those roles required me to sleepwalk through them because I had the appreciation as an actor. I was sadly mistaken because everything you do on screen, even sleeping on the screen, has to be done convincingly. You can't do it, thinking—*Arrey, kisiko kya pata chalega?*'

For *The Dirty Picture* she tried out more than two hundred costumes and danced to Hindi music from the eighties till she was absolutely comfortable with the dance steps and began enjoying it. 'I remember the first day we put on the song "Oo Mungda Mungda" [from the film *Inkaar*, 1977] and danced, I thought that if I could not do it there [in the studio before the shooting started] I would never be able to. I pushed the boundaries on every front. I let myself go with the pelvic thrusts and the bosom heaving. I totally let my hair down,' she says.

And while the actress makes the process sound very simple, the truth is that it takes a lot of courage to make the shift. After all, putting a well-accepted and popular image on the line is the biggest risk for an actor. But Balan did not hesitate. To personify Silk in *The Dirty Picture*, she piled on the pounds and worked on her dancing skills. Being a trained classical dancer, she had never danced with such abandon before; yet, Balan made it all look very believable.

In fact, even during the making of her film *Kahaani* (the story of a pregnant woman looking for her husband), she started the process of getting under the skin of the character long before shooting commenced, keeping a prosthetic belly tied to her so that she would get the 'walk' right. She even forbade director Sujoy Ghosh and crew members from smoking around her!

Balan's diligence in developing the character resulted in a fine work of cinema, catapulting her to dizzying heights of fame. Occasionally, it is important to be obsessed with the job at hand in order to come out with flying colours. Balan's seriousness about getting every little nuance right has become the method to her success.

Each situation brings a fresh set of challenges; it is important to meet them head on and make your own rules, as the actress has consistently done.

CRITICAL ANALYSIS

'Few people have the wisdom to prefer the criticism that would do them good, to the praise that deceives them.'
—*FRANCOIS DE LA ROCHEFOUCAULD*

When there is intense criticism, people tend to either shape up or ship out. Balan first took care to understand the reasons for the flak she got. She reviewed her position to figure out where her fault lay, and pinpointed it to taking her success for granted and trying to fit in with the stereotype instead of playing to her strengths. This effort to correctly analyse and process the feedback that was directed at her played a huge role in turning her career around.

According to the actress, 'During that time I had a lot of definitive conversations, and one was with my brother-in-law Kedar. I was down and out, because I thought I had made it, and then everything was slipping from my hands. He asked me why I had joined films and I said I wanted to live different people's lives on screen. I told him that I was not comfortable if I didn't have a definitive character to play. Maybe I was trying to justify myself but it made things clearer in my own mind. So, that's the biggest lesson I learnt when I went through all that criticism for doing indifferent work. There was criticism about the clothes; there was criticism about *Heyy Babyy*, criticism on pretty much everything. At that time it is [sic] difficult to digest. In trying to fit in and not making any effort in the right direction, I was sticking out like a sore thumb.'

Balan set to work constructively—instead of signing up more projects that offered her uni-dimensional glam-doll roles, she began focusing on films that gave her the option of playing well-etched characters. And the result was there for all to see. Within a short span of about eight years, she nailed all the major film awards (Screen Awards included), besides bagging the most delectable roles in the film industry, making each of them memorable.

Criticism, Balan discovered, had forced her back in the right direction. Until the time she was able to identify where she was going wrong, she was merely drifting from one indifferent role to another.

EMBRACE YOURSELF

'There is nothing more beautiful than seeing a person being themselves. Imagine going through your day being unapologetically you.'—STEVE MARABOLI

Since the beginning of her career, Balan's roles have reinforced her Indianness. Off-screen too, the style that works best for her is traditional Indian wear. 'I have worn Indian clothes forever.

It's like second skin for me. It also compliments the way I am made—facially and physically,' says Balan.

In present times, when women in general and actresses in particular prune themselves to fit the Western body template, Balan stands out as a shining example of Indian individuality. She reminds one of the elegant simplicity of Hindi cinema, best symbolized by the ladies in the Hrishikesh Mukherjee/Basu Chatterjee middle-of-the-road films of the 1970s and '80s. Or even the parallel cinema actresses of those times, in terms of the brave roles she has chosen. She has forged ahead by employing the leitmotif of the conventional Indian woman to essay the unconventional, and that has been a huge part of her success.

'Among actresses who had a lasting impression on me are Jaya Bachchan and Shabana Azmi. Jayaji is an actress who was fantastic at what she did but was also a commercial success and that is the position one would strive for,' confesses Balan, who has been compared to Waheeda Rehman by Amitabh Bachchan himself!

During the making of *Paa*, Balan met designer Sabyasachi Mukherjee, with whose help she rediscovered the humble sari in its many hues. Critics accuse her of playing it safe by sticking to Kanjeevarams and cottons, but by keeping her own counsel, Balan has endeared herself to thousands of women across India who actually wear saris as a matter of course.

In embracing and carrying herself with confidence both on and off screen, Vidya Balan sends out a strong message of retaining one's individuality.

BE BOLD

*'Labels are for filing. Labels are for clothing.
Labels are not for people.'*—MARTINA NAVRATILOVA

Success has emboldened Balan positively. She has started picking up interesting projects and shouldering the responsibility of good films, even if their financial future is uncertain. When he approached her for *Kahaani*, director Sujoy Ghosh had just delivered his second flop film, *Aladin* (2009). A heroine-centric project was risky. No financier had come on board till then; Balan went ahead with it because she liked the story. The results are there for all to see. Considering the amount of time she had invested in the project, it was a huge risk. But it reaped better dividends than the films where she had played safe!

Balan stands tall as someone who took a good hard look at her own self before abandoning the beaten track in order to carve her own path. And, in this process, she has become a shining example of reinvention.

REINVENT THE WHEEL, THE VIDYA BALAN WAY

Vidya Balan's dazzling career span has inspired multitudes of women. An impressive turnaround, all on her own terms. Not to mention how she single-handedly threw out the size-zero bane for both actresses and women in general. She has proved that good girls don't always finish last; they can, and do come first.

- ☆ **Success secret:** You can't take success for granted, a mistake Balan made in the early part of her career. When the going was good, doing more of the same without analysing what had worked in her favour was a natural progression. However, after a certain period of time, her choices caught up and, much to her chagrin, she was compelled to reassess the situation. In the film industry, where success is worshipped, it is easy to be short-sighted. Failure, on the other hand, can teach the harder, more valuable lessons.
- ☆ **Skip stereotypes:** After the initial euphoria had settled down, Balan was eager and willing to fit into the mould of the typical Hindi film heroine, the girl who dolls up and prances around. While the glamorous image has worked its magic for several leading actresses of her generation, it just didn't do the trick for her. For Balan, the shoes of a glam-doll were an awkward fit. Fortunately, the criticism such roles evoked stopped her in her tracks and having corrected her mistake, she broke the mould.

- ☆ **Analyse this:** Among the most significant aspects of Balan's turnaround story is her ability to revisit her failures and accept criticism positively. The actress made a genuine effort to understand where the problem lay, not just by discussing the problem with her family members but also by taking steps to address those issues, once they were identified. An ability to examine and analyse facts objectively is a great boon in showbiz, where judgment can be clouded due to the flattery and attention that comes with the job. The honest self-analysis gave her clarity about the kind of work she wanted to do.
- ☆ **Play to your strengths:** While experimentation is good, it pays to identify and fortify your strengths. Most ambitious people like to push boundaries in all that they do, but nobody can do everything perfectly. There are some things one can do better than others. This awareness helps one's cause, as it did Balan's. She recognized her ability to play challenging and meaty roles, a feat not everyone can pull off. It also helped that the audience liked her portrayals as a woman of substance. And since that realization, there has been no looking back.

AAMIR KHAN
Pursuit of Perfection

'Pleasure in the job puts perfection in the work.'

—ARISTOTLE

During his visit to India in February 2013, British Prime Minister David Cameron requested Aamir Khan's company when he met with students of the Janki Devi Memorial College in Delhi. This unexpected choice was on account of Aamir's association with education—he had been part of the Teach India initiative (run by *The Times of India*) following his film *Taare Zameen Par* (2007), about a dyslexic child, and his television show *Satyamev Jayate* (2012–), based on social issues.

On an earlier occasion, then US Secretary of State Hillary Clinton had met with the superstar. In April 2013, US President Barack Obama and his wife Michelle invited Khan for the President's Dinner in the US, perhaps the outcome of Khan being featured rather prominently on the cover of *Time* magazine as one of the world's most influential people. He was also profiled in *Variety*, America's oldest and most trusted film business publication, as the 'International Star to Know', clearly suggesting that the actor, producer, director, television host and now something of a social vigilante is Bollywood's most wanted superstar!

This high-power itinerary is the outcome of an impressive line-up of films and a television show produced under his banner, Aamir Khan Productions. Khan holds a unique place in Bollywood as he, by dint of excellence in his line of work, has impacted multitudes. Sample this: *Taare Zameen Par* sensitized viewers to children with special needs, *3 Idiots* (2009) taught them to chase excellence not success, while *Peepli (Live)* (2010) raised awareness about disenfranchisement of poor farmers. And *Satyamev Jayate*, his famous television show, reminded us of 'shining' India's ugly truths.

Aamir Khan, more than any other film personality, has employed cinema both to engage and entertain and television to create social awareness. In the bargain, he given Bollywood its 100-crore profit benchmark! No wonder, when it comes to achieving excellence and perfection, he is the film industry's favourite example. Let us walk through the methods that catapulted him to this enviable position.

SMART THINKING

'Thinking. The talking of the soul with itself.'—PLATO

Aamir Khan has a penchant for turning convention on its head—he dares to step into unchartered territories, though not without caution. A thumb rule he follows at all times is to not rush into things. After all, as they say, 'Fools rush in where angels fear to tread.'

Superstar, producer and director with a career spanning over twenty-five years and an array of impressive performances, Khan has acquired the enviable tag of Mr Perfectionist—an intellectual superstar and a new-age genius—by sheer hard work, smart thinking and unwavering devotion to the cause of creating perfect cinema. Cinema that is engaging, yet commercially sustainable.

Ask anyone who has worked with Khan and they will tell you about how painstakingly he examines the pros and cons of any project offered to him before giving his nod. The waiting period could run into weeks, months or years, depending on how much the idea appeals to him and how busy he is at that point of time. The story of *Lagaan* was related to Khan four times before he finally decided to produce it! Friend and director Ashutosh Gowariker, who had written the script, had to go back to the drawing board repeatedly before the project was green-lit. In an interview to film-maker Asif Kapadia in

> For Aamir Khan Productions every film is a challenge. We pick up something unusual and weird and I often think ke bana toh diya hai, but who is going to watch it? The fear is always there but it doesn't stop me from doing what I want. I would like to pick unusual films that nobody else is making and do path-breaking work. I hope I have the courage to keep doing that, and, in that also lies our growth. When you challenge yourself you grow.

The Guardian, Khan mentions that even on hearing a revised version that he'd liked, he'd requested Gowariker to narrate the story to him once more in the company of his parents and then wife Reena. While the director did so, Khan watched the faces of his family members keenly for their reactions. Only after he was convinced that all of them (including his father, a seasoned producer) had enjoyed hearing the story did he agree to sign it.

Work on *Peepli (Live)*, a social satire on media and the plight of poor farmers, a story he liked immensely, started almost four years after it was first narrated to him by director Anusha Rizvi. But once convinced, Khan is willing to go the whole mile as he did with both *Lagaan* and *Peepli (Live)*, by donning the producer's mantle.

Thinking through the pros and cons is something everybody speaks of, but very few practise. A true analysis of a project's viability can be brutal to those deeply involved with it. But a full and frank assessment is the only way forward, even if it takes up a significant amount of time. Khan's success shows that intense evaluation followed by absolute dedication is the surest road to success.

OUT-OF-THE-BOX IDEAS

'To create a new standard, you have to be up for that challenge and really enjoy it.'—SHIGERU MIYAMOTO

Qayamat Se Qayamat Tak (1988), Khan's first film, was a runaway hit; overnight he turned into a superstar. But it was the after-period that hinted at what was in store vis-à-vis this new kid on the block.

What came across clearly was his penchant for picking up unusual subjects like the art film *Raakh* (1989), about a rape victim and her boyfriend's attempt to avenge her humiliation. Then there were films such as *Awwal Number* (1990; cricket against the backdrop of terror threats), *Jo Jeeta Wohi Sikander* (1992; one of those exceptionally entertaining films wherein a cycling race was the high point, as opposed to Bollywood's staple formula of romance), *Hum Hain Rahi Pyar Ke* (1993; a love story which had Khan play guardian to four kids—risky for a young actor), which even in the early part of his career, stood out for their 'different' content.

Not all these films boasted grand earnings or critical acclaim, but it was evident that as an actor, Khan had an exceptional bent of mind. His choice of films was unconventional in the early 1990s, when middle-of-the-road multiplex cinema had not yet found favour with the audience or the film industry.

In addition to trying out ideas that were 'different', he was equally open to working with new talent then, as he is today, after establishing his superstar status. Why, Khan's debut film *Qayamat Se Qayamat Tak* was directed by his first cousin Mansoor Khan, a newbie himself! Besides newcomers, he has also worked with directors like Ashutosh Gowariker and Rakeysh Omprakash Mehra, who previously had unsuccessful films on their resume, signing up on the sheer basis of a good idea and the enthusiasm to work hard. Their films together, *Lagaan* and *Rang de Basanti* (2006) respectively, went on to become huge commercial and critical successes. His recent projects—*Dhobi Ghat* (2010), *Peepli (Live)* and *Delhi Belly* (2011) among others—were directed by first-timers. 'For me, names don't matter. I am happy to be a platform that supports young talent,' he once said. 'For Aamir Khan Productions every film is a challenge. We pick up something unusual and weird and I often think ke bana toh diya hai, but who is going to watch it? The fear is always there but it doesn't stop me from doing what I want. I would like to pick unusual films that nobody else is making and do path-breaking work. I hope I have the courage to keep doing that, and, in that also lies our growth. When you challenge yourself you grow.'

Having the ability to take risks and roll with the punches is developed through astute observation of one's environment. Khan's understanding is that no one really knows what works, but by believing firmly in one's decisions, one can even make the seemingly impossible idea bear fruit.

CHOOSING WITH CARE

'If one remains as careful at the end as he was at the beginning, there will be no failure.'—LAO TZU

As the story goes, Khan was the original choice for *Darr* (1993), which eventually went to Shah Rukh Khan. Given that it was a two-hero film, Khan asked for joint narrations with Sunny Deol, the other male lead of the film, and was consequently shown the door by industry veteran Yash Chopra, the director of the film. But this incident did not compel the actor to change his ways. He continues to question and think things through till he is absolutely convinced of its merit. The only difference since then is that he is now lauded for it. In fact, he was later a part of *Fanaa* (2006) and *Dhoom 3* (2013), two productions of Chopra's Yash Raj Films.

> I am sure, I have drawbacks like everyone but I am hard on myself and everyone else because we have a responsibility to the audience and ourselves. You have to do what is right, even if it is not good for you personally. And you have to do it as well as possible.

When asked about taking up a role in *Dhobi Ghat*, his wife Kiran Rao's film, Khan put this cautious approach in perspective and said, 'I am very protective of myself and what I get attached to (creatively). If I didn't like the script of *Dhobi Ghat*, I would not have done it. I would have been supportive of Kiran's effort as a husband, taken her out for a dinner after a hectic day at shoot. But I would not have involved myself professionally.

'Film-making is very tough and demanding, it takes a lot from you. For me to give so much to a film, it has to be worthwhile. In other words, the process has to make me happy and that is what drives me. Like my character Rancho from the film *3 Idiots*, I am not aiming for success. I am able to do work that makes me happy and success has followed.'

The choices one makes shape one's future. Caution and an astute understanding of the environment are needed to make good decisions that aid one's growth. Khan has worked towards this understanding, turning it into an instinct, and in the process, grown from strength to strength.

DEVIL LIES IN THE DETAILS

*'It's the little details that are vital.
Little things make big things happen.'*—JOHN WOODEN

True to his reputation, when Aamir Khan takes up a project, he ensures that it is impeccably executed. It has even created a myth about the actor ghost-directing all the films he becomes part of. His middle innings was marked by peeved directors such as Mahesh Bhatt (*Dil Hai Ki Manta Nahin,* 1991) and Ram Gopal Varma (*Rangeela*, 1995) who cited creative interference from the actor. Over a period of time, though, he has earned grudging admiration from the film industry, including even the above-mentioned directors. Film-maker Rajkumar Hirani, who collaborated with him on *3 Idiots*, along with a whole new generation of directors like Rakeysh Omprakash Mehra, think of Khan's involvement as a definite plus, as it substantially improves the film's creative quality and commercial prospects.

This involvement extends beyond the film-making process. With *Lagaan*, Khan was involved at all levels, both as a producer and actor. On the sets, he would sit around in the sun wearing a dhoti to get a natural tan for the role of a peasant! When the film was entered for the Academy Awards in the Best Foreign Film category, the actor parked himself in Los Angeles, ensuring that members of the Academy got to watch the film in order to better its chances. As it turns out, *Lagaan* made its way into the nominations, only the third Indian film then to do so.

It has been no different with the rest of his films. For *Delhi Belly* and *Peepli (Live)*, films that he produced, he participated in the editing, a very significant and tedious aspect of film-making, to ensure that the films lived up to their promise. Few stars, even when they are producing the film, have the patience to sit beyond the negotiations or promotions. No wonder then that Khan's determined diligence always results in superior content, no matter what the genre.

Attention to detail can make a project, while the lack of it can result in a disaster. Many an artist has fallen by the wayside for relying just on talent. Khan's conviction that talent is 99 per cent perspiration and involvement in getting each little aspect right has taken him ahead by leaps and bounds.

AUDITION FOR THE PART

'Success or failure in business is caused more by the mental attitude even than by mental capacities.'—WALTER SCOTT

Anyone familiar with standard practices in Bollywood would know that lead stars never audition for the part. It is usually character actors who go through the process. An anomaly to this rule is the perfectionist Khan, who auditioned for his part in Kiran Rao's film *Dhobi Ghat*. According to Rao, he was the last one to be signed up, that too only after both of them were convinced that he was pitch perfect for playing a reclusive painter.

The rule extends to all family members, be it wife Kiran or nephew Imran Khan, whom he's immensely fond of. Despite their strong family association, Khan insisted on Imran's auditioning for the lead role in *Jaane Tu Ya Jaane Na* (2008), which turned out to be a stupendous hit, pole-vaulting Imran into the big

> It's not just about doing good things but about doing them well.

league. *Dhobi Ghat* too received rave reviews at the Toronto International Film Festival and even back home.

'Suitability for the part, that's the first thing. If you see our casting, we have not really gone for stars. Even if I have to do it myself, I screen-test. If I don't suit a part, I am not in it. I am sure, I have drawbacks like everyone but I am hard on myself and everyone else because we have a responsibility to the audience and ourselves. You have to do what is right, even if it is not good for you personally. And you have to do it as well as possible,' Khan says.

'Horses for courses' is an oft-bandied phrase, but making sure that the horse is a racehorse and not a pony is what makes the difference between success and failure. In Khan's case he makes sure that whether an actor or technician, friend or acquaintance, he will only get the right person for the job.

FORGE YOUR OWN PATH

'Do not go where the path may lead, go instead where there is no path and leave a trail.'—RALPH WALDO EMERSON

This is a motto that the actor has lived by—working with newcomers being a small part of it. Both the trajectory and Khan's working style don't have precedence, though now they are widely emulated by the new lot. But he was the only actor of his generation to work in one film at a time, spending considerable effort in getting the look and feel of the character right. As early as 1994, when he was working on three or four films together, he decided to step back and work in just one film exclusively.

'I love my work very much and every time I take on an endeavour, I have to live with the fear of it going wrong or failing. But this fear keeps me alert. It keeps me going and I don't allow it to change my decisions,' explained Khan at Express Adda. Every time a risky idea came up, he took ownership of it and put his money where his mouth was. During the filming of *Lagaan*, when the crew was running late and schedules had gone awry, the actor and first-time producer would often wonder if he had bitten off more than he could chew. But whenever the going got tough, he would remember a scene from the film.

'In *Lagaan* there is a scene when the villagers are not doing too well as a team, and my character Bhuvan asks his mother, *"Maa ee bida utha ke maine koi galti to nahin ki?"* (Did I make a mistake by taking on this challenge?). It's happened with all my films but each time I have followed my heart. The reality is that the market moves towards safer options. The market would want me to do a *Dilwale Dulhaniya Le Jayenge* but every time I do a *Taare Zameen Par*, the market looks at me with suspicion. I am a star but even I have had to fight suspicion about almost every film,' avers the star, hinting at battles he has fought in the larger interest of creativity.

To take bold steps in an environment which thrives on sticking to the tried and tested is the hardest thing to do. But as a consummate creative mind, Khan lives by the idiom: nothing ventured, nothing gained.

CREATE A BUZZ

'Nothing except the mint can make money without advertising.'
—THOMAS B. MACAULAY

Among Khan's numerous achievements in cinema is the importance he gives to marketing a film, a commercial aspect that he has honed into a fine art. In fact, the superstar has been hailed as something of a marketing genius. He was even invited to the Indian Institute of Management, Ahmedabad, for a guest lecture on films. He generated great curiosity for his film *Ghajini* (2008) when he gave cinema ushers and some of his fans a 'Ghajini' haircut, similar to the look he was sporting in the film. Photos in the newspapers of the superstar shearing men's crowning glory created an instant curiosity around the film, which went on to become a 100-crore hit! As part of its publicity campaign, Khan also sent every journalist that he had interacted with a personalized mail with a short note of his first impression/memory of the person in question. This was a clever promotional ploy, since *Ghajini* was a revenge saga about a man suffering from partial memory loss!

For *3 Idiots*, Khan was a regular on social networking sites Twitter, Facebook and Orkut to interact with the young students frequenting these sites. He even 'disappeared' for a while, as his character in the movie does, making sudden appearances in towns all over India, asking his fans to guess where he would appear next. As far as Khan is concerned it's all quite simple, 'The biggest marketing you can ever do for yourself is good work. I can't mislead the audience with whom I have had a relationship spanning twenty years. When marketing [a film], I have to be totally honest with them about the kind of film we have made and let them decide whether they want to watch it or not.'

A campaign can only be successful if the idea sold lives up to its potential. Honesty of thought is therefore integral to Khan's unique brand of marketing. These are the marketing mantras that Khan swears by, and time and again they bring home results, creating widespread awareness about his work.

OBSERVE AND LEARN

'I have got a theory that if you give 100 per cent all of the time, somehow things will work out in the end.'—LARRY BIRD

'It's not just about doing good things but about doing them well' is the motto of superstar Aamir Khan.

To Khan goes the credit for introducing a 360-degree approach to creating good films. Renowned scriptwriter, lyricist and poet Javed Akhtar once remarked that Khan, more than any other actor, had a holistic sense of cinema and an unerring eye for detail that others lacked.

In a book about him, *I'll Do It My Way* by Christina Daniels, I read that the seeds of this deep-rooted focus were sown in his childhood, as he would listen to film narrations by writers and directors pitching their stories to his father Tahir Hussain and uncle Nasir Hussain, something that later helped him identify good scripts.

For the longest time, actors were content working on their scenes, getting their lines right, performing their stunts or keeping step with the choreographer, till Khan burst on to the scene. Not only did he work on all of the above, he was also involved with the narrative structure, editing, promotional strategies and so on. As mentioned in an article in *Mid-day*, a city tabloid, after his film *Qayamat Se Qayamat Tak* released, Khan would go into the projection room of the Gaiety Galaxy film theatre in Bandra to observe the audience's reaction during various scenes. He would carefully witness the parts that elicited laughter and the bits when people stepped out for 'toilet visits'.

When Khan decided to turn director with *Taare Zameen Par*, he had his work cut out—he was actor, director and producer all rolled into one. So, during his test screenings, he was utterly dismayed when the point he was trying to make about Nikumbh Sir, the art teacher (who too had suffered from dyslexia and was therefore able to grasp the child protagonist's problem), was lost on his test audience. However, instead of giving up, he spoke to them at length and realized that a change in the sequence of shots would help get the point across. He implemented the changes, and the outcome was a thought-provoking and poignant film about children. The result of his all-round efforts has been spectacular, with an almost 100 per cent success ratio as far as Aamir Khan Productions is concerned.

Usually people are content just getting their work done, but not Khan, whose attempt has always been to understand and gauge whether the job has been done well enough or not. By seeking out a cross-section of reactions to his work, he is able to fine-tune it, so that its approval by a critical mass of consumers is more or less assured.

AAMIR'S PERFECTION DECODED

In his long career, Aamir Khan has established himself as a creative force to reckon with. Experimental and brave, he is extremely committed to his craft; it is hardly surprising that as a producer, he has had a 100 per cent strike rate. Even when his film is not a blockbuster it usually ensures profits for people in the distribution chain. Along with creative responsibility, he takes the onus of ensuring a safe budget for the films according to the subject and probable appeal. Unlike several contemporaries, he keeps away from creative indulgence, driving himself as hard as the rest of his team. That is why he is known as Mr Perfectionist. Here is how a constant pursuit of perfection works wonders for the superstar.

☆ **Litmus test:** Among the first actors of his generation to try out crowd testing of films long before their release, Khan has created an almost foolproof way of spotting the common creative mistakes that people are prone to make. And while he is very open to opinions and suggestions, it is largely to gauge whether the idea that he is trying to convey is being communicated effectively. If not, he does not change the message; he merely tweaks the method of communication. In a creative industry such practice is considered high risk, but it has reaped great results for him.

☆ **Experiments with truth:** In trying out new ideas and new talent, Khan has strengthened himself as a canny creative force. His television show *Satyamev Jayate* was among the bold new ideas on television, wherein a superstar was presenting something that was not an entertainment, reality or game show, but touched upon social issues such as female infanticide and medical malpractices. The response, despite modest TRPs, was tremendous and it immediately catapulted his popularity, enhancing his international profile. He was featured on the cover of *Time* magazine, besides being written about in *The New York Times,* along with several other international publications, for shining the spotlight on social issues.

☆ **Planned moves:** Where several stars adopt a gladiator approach to their craft, banking heavily on their superstar prowess, Khan functions like a strategist, a chess player carefully thinking through his moves. His ability to study, understand and therefore pre-empt pitfalls makes even his experimental projects appear risk-free.

☆ **Lay down the law:** A considerable part of Khan's success lies in an inherent honesty of approach. The star clearly spells out the rules, fine print included, to those who wish to work with him. Director Amol Gupte, who wrote *Taare Zameen Par,* was pencilled in to direct the film, but when Khan was unhappy with what had been shot, he gave Gupte the option to walk out of the project. It was mutually decided that the superstar would direct the film while Gupte would be compensated and given due credit for the story. And Khan kept his word. Such clarity and integrity of intent strengthens his reputation of being fair and professional, giving him and his company an edge in drawing creative talent from different walks of life.

KATRINA KAIF

Perseverance

'Patience and perseverance have a magical effect before which difficulties disappear and obstacles vanish.'

—John Quincy Adams

Better known as the hit machine of the film industry, Katrina Kaif, one of the most beautiful and popular actresses of Hindi cinema, made it to Bollywood's top echelons after a decade of toil, to live a dream that most can only aspire for. Not only is she among the most searched-for actresses on the Internet, but according to an annual survey conducted in 2009 by *Screen*, she's also the female star that people most desire to watch among the popular actresses in contemporary Bollywood!

What are the odds that a young girl from Britain who knew no Hindi, and was of mixed parentage (her father is Kashmiri while her mother is British) would find her way to superstardom in Bollywood? All within a short span of eight years? It could well be a chapter from Ripley's *Believe It or Not*!

Blessed with stunning looks, a career in the movies seemed a natural choice for Kaif, who spent a large part of her childhood in cities such as Hong Kong and London, among others. She was modelling in London when director Kaizad Gustad signed her up for his film *Boom* (2003). The film bombed, but the PYT was snapped up for various modelling assignments in India. About two years later, in 2005, she returned to an acting career, this time more resolutely with *Maine Pyaar Kyun Kiya* (2005) and *Sarkar* (2005).

Initially, the newcomer was dismissed as just a pretty face, probably no more than a footnote in

> Everybody works hard. With me the difference is that my film becomes an obsession at that time so it could be anything—what's happening on the set, what is the assistant director doing, what kind of vibe should it have; I have always wanted to be a part of the whole thing.

Hindi cinema, but Kaif, with her dedication and perseverance, proved the experts completely wrong. A decade later, after playing a major part in some very successful films such as *Welcome* (2007), *Partner* (2007), *Namastey London* (2007), *Singh is Kinng* (2008), *Race* (2008), *New York* (2009), *Raajneeti* (2010), *Mere Brother Ki Dulhan* (2011), *Zindagi Na Milegi Dobara* (2011), *Ek Tha Tiger* (2012) and *Dhoom 3* (2013), she is very much around and going strong. In fact, in *Screen's* annual survey for 2013, she received the maximum votes for the actress who has the greatest brand value.

That her leading men, some of whom were her mentors, now request to have her in their films, even if it's only for a song, is testimony to Kaif's impressive resilience and her rise. Kaif's combination of hard work and smart choices has won her the coveted crown of being Bollywood's most wanted.

Here's how she made it happen for herself.

WORK IT UP

'To pay attention, this is our endless and proper work.'
—MARY OLIVER

Hard-working is an adjective used very often when colleagues describe Katrina Kaif, but it's not just about hard work. Her dedication to the work at hand is exemplary. I remember the first time we met up for an interview—the multi-starrer *Welcome* was to release; she had rushed back from a shoot abroad for the promotion of the film and was diligently doing her share of press interviews. Any other day, it would have been an oft-followed routine, but Kaif's dedication stood out because coincidentally, the interviews had been scheduled on Salman Khan's birthday (they were dating at the time). Celebrations were in order and yet there she was, doing her bit towards promoting the film.

When reminded of the incident, she said, 'My involvement is a lot—the film you are referring to was not the most hyped film and required promotion. The director and the entire team had worked so hard on it, so it would not be fair, to not promote it. Everybody works hard. With me the difference is that my film becomes an obsession at that time so it could be anything—what's happening on the set, what is the assistant director doing, what kind of vibe should it have; I have always wanted to be a part of the whole thing.'

The distance between involvement and hard work is a fine one, but the right measure makes a huge difference to the outcome. Kaif's ability to combine both has worked wonders for her career. Not only does she work hard to get things right but ensures that she also understands the requirements of the job at hand. This guarantees that all efforts are well-utilized.

FLEXI-MIND

'Let no one think that flexibility and a predisposition to compromise is a sign of weakness or a sell-out.'—PAUL KAGAME

When she began shooting for Subhash Ghai's *Yuvvraaj* (2008), Kaif was just three years old in the film industry. But during the filming of a song, when the director asked her to prance and pirouette around a stairway, she heard him out quietly before asking if she could temper down the action by a notch or two for the shot. The director stuck to his opinion and the song went on to be filmed as per his instructions. What is interesting is that even as a newcomer, Kaif was brave enough to articulate her opinion to a veteran director, as she feels that in cinematic collaborations, it is important to share thoughts and ideas. However, she was not adamant about her idea and went ahead with the way the director had envisioned the scene without starry tantrums.

'I would never enforce my opinion but I have them [sic]. Movie-making is a collaborative effort so an actor has to bring alive the character and you need the director to guide what you are doing. You have to give suggestions and the director will reject or accept but from my experience, I have found that the most successful partnerships usually come when the director and actor have a very good dialogue,' says Kaif.

The good news is that occasionally her views get accepted too! As was the case with *Jab Tak Hai Jaan* (2012); Shah Rukh Khan ceded ground to Kaif in a scene wherein he had to recite the lines of a poem in a particular fashion.

A flexible approach to work and situations is a boon that is highly underrated. It is key to being accepted in teams—someone who is hassle-free and willing to accept other people's leadership is always welcomed in group initiatives. Kaif's ability to hold her opinions and yet not be didactic makes her easy to work with. She also benefits by trying out different suggestions, thus broadening her horizons.

NO SHORTCUTS

*'When it comes to success,
there are no shortcuts.'*—BO BENNETT

'Who wants to look bad?' is Kaif's matter-of-fact quip when complimented on her ability and willingness to rehearse, be it a scene, dance moves or a live performance. The ability to dance like a pro is a must-have skill for all of Bollywood's leading ladies, and twirling in sky-high heels and flouncy gowns with elaborate hairdos is certainly not an easy task. Since Kaif grew up largely in the West, with minimal exposure to Bollywood, it was difficult for her in the beginning. 'Sure it was awkward, for instance, there is a dance sequence and you are completely out of your depth. You don't know what you are doing! But that's also the fun in life, trying out things, realising you are bad and then getting better. Teaching yourself, improving...I think that's the fun part of the journey,' she avers.

In the early years, Kaif was at the lower end of the pecking order during live performances (less established stars perform first) but now she is the lead attraction, with all major event organizers vying to get her on board. Among leading actresses, she has the maximum number of hit songs with tricky moves to her credit—'Sheila ki Jawani' from *Tees Maar Khan* (2010), 'Chikni Chameli' from *Agneepath* (2012) and 'Mashallah' from *Ek Tha Tiger*, to name a few. Quite impressive for someone who was considered stiff at the outset!

Talking of the struggle to get it right, the actress avers, '"Chikni Chameli" saw us working hard for thirteen hours a day and going back all exhausted. When it comes to dance, yes, I rehearse a lot. I love dancing but I hate the first day of rehearsals. I get into depression, and think everything looks awful and bad. The second day sees things getting a little better. On the third day I find my rhythm.'

According to co-star and friend Salman Khan, 'Katrina is very hardworking. For every intricate movement in the song[s] [for *Ek Tha Tiger*], she would insist on getting it right. If she knows there is a deadline, she will work those extra hours and get the steps right.'

There are a lot of things that one may aspire for and then put aside because they seem unattainable. The road to success is often a rough one. Kaif, however, saw the hard work required for the job as a challenge. She plunged right into the song-and-dance routine of Hindi films, totally out of her comfort zone. Realizing how important dancing skills are for a Hindi movie heroine, she worked on them tirelessly. Her ability and willingness to rehearse helps her pull off some of the most difficult dance sequences. It has certainly added tremendously to her popularity.

> I have worked with really good people, so with everyone I have observed and picked up little things. Like Akshay's work ethic. He was the first one to talk to me about how someone has to approach the industry, the hours, the preparation etc.

NEWER GOALPOSTS

'I don't run away from a challenge because I am afraid. Instead, I run toward it because the only way to escape fear is to trample it beneath your foot.'—NADIA COMANECI

Kaif confesses to being restless. She sets herself short-term goals, which once accomplished propel her to move on to a whole new set of goals. According to her, 'I am a very restless person in that way, when I have achieved the goals I set, my mind starts wandering towards new challenges.'

She began her career as a model and once she had achieved her goal of landing prestigious modelling assignments, a

> I know exactly what I have or have not achieved even if the movie is a hit. So having said that, yes, even though I have been very fortunate that most of my movies have done well, when I am going to sleep at night or sitting by myself during the day, I know in my heart, what I have, or haven't achieved. It's not like I sit on a cloud and say, 'It doesn't matter or I don't care.'

full-fledged Bollywood career seemed like the obvious challenge to sign up for.

But a major obstacle lay in Kaif's path—the fact that she could not even speak Hindi! Since she had lived in Hong Kong and England for a substantial part of her childhood, she initially had some difficulty with Hindi dialogues. Her lines were even dubbed for a couple of films, but Kaif was not one to lose heart. She learnt on the job. She also hired a tutor to teach her to read the Devanagari script and converse in Hindi, till she became fluent enough to deliver her own dialogues with a flourish.

When shooting for Prakash Jha's *Raajneeti* (2010), Kaif learnt her chaste, highbrow Hindi dialogues by typing them out on her phone so that she could memorize the lines.

It is this zealous nature that has seen her grow from strength to strength. From co-star Salman Khan's home production *Maine Pyaar Kyun Kiya* in which she landed the Barbie-doll part, to becoming Akshay Kumar's lead actress in several films such as *Welcome, Namastey London* and *Singh is Kinng* to a film—*Mere Brother Ki Dulhan*—where she had the central role, equal to those of co-stars Imran Khan and Ali Zafar, Kaif's progress has been impressive.

Now, after establishing herself as a competent actress who can carry off romantic films with elan and dance like a dream, Kaif has trained her sights on becoming an action expert, after her stunts in *Ek Tha Tiger* earned her praise. For *Dhoom 3*, she underwent extensive physical training and even though some of the stunts left her bruised all over, she signed up for *Bang Bang* (forthcoming[*]), one more action film!

More often than not, once a goal is achieved, we settle down to the comfort of routine. After all, taking up a new challenge means starting from scratch and working hard all over again. Katrina Kaif's eagerness to venture into new, unexplored areas even if it means tremendous hard work ensures that she does not stagnate in a creative job.

KNOW YOURSELF

'It's difficult to appreciate the value of others when your own assessment is overvalued.'—ANONYMOUS

'I do feel that I have made some safe choices but I don't regret it because they were necessary at that time,' was Kaif's reply to my question on picking projects that were high on the glamour quotient in the early part of her career.

In the beginning, Kaif chose her films cautiously—she was mostly seen in glamour-girl roles with a few songs. More often than not, she was either an NRI or a girl who was educated in a foreign university, to justify her British accent.

Those were smart choices based on an astute assessment of her strengths and weaknesses at that time. She was wise to

---
[*]At the time of writing

pick films that had her play second fiddle to the hero in the early part of her career, when she was unfamiliar with the nuances of acting in Hindi films. With just basic knowledge of the language, it made sense to pick roles wherein glamour was the mainstay.

'Regardless of the success and failure of a film, I have a very clear-cut idea of exactly what has been achieved or not achieved with that particular film. I am very self-critical and self-aware, I should say.

'I know exactly what I have or have not achieved even if the movie is a hit. So having said that, yes, even though I have been very fortunate that most of my movies have done well, when I am going to sleep at night or sitting by myself during the day, I know in my heart, what I have, or haven't achieved. It's not like I sit on a cloud and say, "It doesn't matter or I don't care."'

Nothing succeeds like success. When a project works well, one just gives oneself a pat on the back and moves on. However, it is important to take stock of the quality of one's performance, regardless of the overall success or failure. Kaif's judgment of her work, both good and bad, is rather sound. Once she assesses herself as falling short, she tries to improve, even if the film had been successful.

GOOD COMPANY

'The key is to keep company only with people who uplift you, whose presence calls forth your best.'—EPICTETUS

Known to be very sensitive by nature, Kaif maintains that she works best in a positive environment, being around people who are encouraging. 'I remember Anil Kapoor teaching me the importance of focusing before a shot. While shooting for *Welcome*, I was playing around in a corner, and he was like, "What are you doing?" I said I was playing to which he said, "I wouldn't, if I were you!"'

Kaif has had the good fortune of working with many successful actors such as Akshay Kumar, Amitabh Bachchan, the three leading Khans: Aamir, Salman and Shah Rukh, (and more if one were to count Imran Khan and Saif Ali Khan), Ranbir Kapoor and John Abraham. Yash Chopra, Kabir Khan and Zoya Akhtar are among the A-list directors who have cast her in their films.

The best part about sharing workspace with a bevy of talented people is getting a ringside view of their superior work skills. As the new kid on the block, Kaif realized the importance of learning on the job by observing veterans at work. Of this unmatched privilege and its virtues, she says, 'I have worked with really good people, so with everyone I have observed and picked up little things. Like Akshay's work ethic. He was the first one to talk to me about how someone has to approach the industry, the hours, the preparation, etc.'

Working sincerely involves learning from the experience of those around us. Katrina Kaif's perseverance extended beyond learning as a drill. Instead of whiling away time on the sets, she spent her time constructively, observing and adhering to advice from seniors about how to approach her work. Often, people undermine the importance of this. As they say, while a wise man learns from others' mistakes, a fool will learn only from his own. Kaif, by making the wiser choice, has turned herself into a winner.

PASS ON THE GOOD DEED

'Possessions, outward success, publicity, luxury—to me, these have always been contemptible. I believe that a simple and unassuming manner of life is best for everyone, best both for the body and mind.'—ALBERT EINSTEIN

Despite touching the pinnacle of her career, Kaif has not forgotten those who helped her in the early stages. Though she is an A-list star and maintains a hectic schedule, she takes out time consistently for returning favours by making guest appearances in films, attending a colleague's birthday party and so on. She has not let the trappings of fame come in the way of personal relationships.

Kaif continues to share a cordial relationship with Salman Khan and his family, and is often a part of their family gatherings, whether it is during Ganpati Puja or private movie screenings. She has always maintained that she is indebted to the entire family for their support and even lends star presence to their films when required. For *Bodyguard* (2011), directed by Siddique, with Salman Khan and Kareena Kapoor in the main roles, Kaif readily agreed to an item song. She also played a small role in co-star Akshay Kumar's film *Blue* (2009).

Being there for people who help you in tough times is the hallmark of a confident and self-assured person. By returning the favour of those who helped her in her initial days, Kaif amply displays her confidence and good grace, increasing her popularity manifold.

KATRINA'S SURE-FOOTED CLIMB TO SUCCESS

That Kaif is the inspiration behind many non-Indian and NRI girls aiming for a Bollywood career is now common knowledge. The climb has been an arduous one with a fair share of highs and lows, but nothing that could not be overcome by her hard work and determination. Let us take a look at Kaif's keys to success:

- ☆ **Compare and contrast:** While comparisons are unavoidable, it is important to understand that you might be in a situation that is completely different from your peers'. Kaif's reality check of her own situation helped her remain grounded. Instead of aping her contemporaries who had a good command over Hindi and more experience in song-and-dance routines and facing the camera, she steered her career in the right direction, assessing her capabilities squarely.
- ☆ **Rome was not built in a day:** An addendum to the earlier point, but a crucial one. Kaif was wise enough to understand that she would not achieve superstardom in a day. Her enviable career graph is the result of years of hard work. As Salman Khan and many others reiterate, success has not made her any less diligent. Even today she will rehearse a dance step till she gets it right. Each success is a small step towards the bigger goal.
- ☆ **Start with the basics:** Unlike most newbies, once Kaif had set her heart on a showbiz career, she began focusing on the crucial and relevant aspects, such as hiring a Hindi tutor and learning to dance. Most others would

have hired a publicist and stylist, in that order, instead of working on their acting.

☆ **Accept good advice:** More often than not, dishing out advice is easier than taking it yourself, but Kaif's ability to put sage counsel from senior co-stars to judicious use has reaped rich dividends for her. From the beginning, whether it was advice from Salman Khan or Akshay Kumar or Vipul Shah about her choice of films and so on, she has adhered to it, with great results.

JOHN ABRAHAM
Enterprise

'You have to learn the rules of the game.
And then you have to play better than anyone else.'

—ALBERT EINSTEIN

Actor, producer and ex-supermodel John Abraham has a few qualities that set him apart from other celebrities. Remembering people, even the most casual of acquaintances, is one. Then, of course, there is the whole fitness bit. The best thing about the Malayali–Parsi Mumbaikar from a middle-class family is that he does not lose heart over failures; he simply learns from them and turns them into opportunities. An avid footballer, John takes immense pride in this sportsman-like attitude.

After ten successful years in the film industry Abraham has notched up thirteen hits—*Jism* (2003), *Dhoom* (2004), *Garam Masala* (2005), *Taxi No. 9211* (2006), *Dostana* (2008), *New York*, *Desi Boys* (2011), *Force* (2011), *Vicky Donor* (2012; as producer), *Housefull 2* (2012), *Shootout at Wadala* (2013), *Race 2* (2013) and *Madras Cafe* (2013), not to forget an international film, *Water* (2005), which was even nominated for the Academy Awards. Considering that he only learnt on the job for the most part, he has scored well. He is the first male supermodel to have catapulted himself to Bollywood's A-list, far ahead of seniors like Deepak Malhotra and Milind Soman, and even contemporaries Arjun Rampal and Dino Morea. Using the fitness plank, Abraham has branched out into sports in a big way—he is the brand ambassador for Mumbai Marathon, Tour de India 2013, besides purchasing a stake in Hockey India League's Delhi Waveriders.

At forty, he is still being tagged the sexiest man alive by *People* magazine (December 2012), among others. Besides being a hugely successful model, actor and producer, he now plans on turning into a fitness entrepreneur, starting with JA fitness centres in Pune, Mumbai and Bangalore.

How did a model without the necessary training or

connections become an A-list film star? The answer lies in the simple values by which he lives his life and his enterprising ways.

CHARM OFFENSIVE

'There is no personal charm so great as the charm of a cheerful temperament.'—HENRY VAN DYKE

In the beginning I had mentioned about Abraham remembering casual acquaintances and even more important, acknowledging them. It is an admirable quality when it comes to winning friends. Why, when I ran into the actor a few years ago at a suburban gym, his cheery greeting of fellow fitness enthusiasts was a pleasant surprise. Abraham is naturally agreeable and pleasant with everyone around. At the said gym, he patiently obliged all fans, even getting photographed with them, after his workout session, of course.

Being polite and courteous is a must, as is humility, though occasionally Abraham does indulge in some cheeky praise of himself. His favourite T-shirt, among those he launched for Wrangler, says, 'I look like John Abraham'. Its origin lies in the countless instances when people told him that he resembles John Abraham! He has also had excited fans tug his hair or poke him in the stomach to check out his fab abs, all of which he takes in his stride. He willingly poses for photographs or signs autographs even after a long, tiring day.

Mentor Maureen Wadia, who discovered him during the Gladrags Manhunt modelling contest, says, 'John is not just about good looks. His humility is what works in his favour.'

A smile goes a mile. Even the most difficult situation

can be made easier if one handles it with cheer and decides to keep cool. Abraham makes sure that he approaches all his prospective producers, directors and business associates with an attitude that says 'even if we don't work together, we can still be friends'. This has won him admirers even among his detractors.

PERTINENT QUESTIONS

'Who questions much, shall learn much and retain much.'
—FRANCIS BACON

My first interview with Abraham is rather vivid in my mind because I recall him (then just a model), asking me a few questions of his own. 'What is the circulation of your magazine?' and then, 'Whom does the magazine go out to? Who are your core readers?'

I was rather surprised at this line of enquiry, and a bit annoyed as well. After all, most models I had interacted with were least interested in such facts. They were happy as long as they were being featured on the cover and clicked by leading fashion photographers. But clearly that was not enough for this upcoming model. I later learnt that he had trained as a media planner in his previous job at an advertising agency; he knew a thing or two about the magazine business, hence

> It's a competitive space and I enjoy it. After all, I am a sportsman.

the questions. He wanted to make sure that the interview with me was time well spent. After all, time is money. Even today, despite his star status, Abraham is curiosity personified, full of questions about facts that may or may not appear pertinent.

Relevant background information is most important. Abraham approaches every interaction armed with basic knowledge about the topic under discussion, at the very least. And if he doesn't, he won't shy away from asking questions on the subject. This helps him make informed decisions, always a plus in any profession.

MAKE IT HAPPEN

'There are people who make things happen, there are people who watch things happen and there are people who wonder what happened. To be successful, you need to be a person who makes things happen.'—JAMES A. LOVELL

To the modelling world, news of Abraham landing and accepting a film offer came as a surprise to most of his work associates because apart from his good looks, he was hardly the quintessential Hindi film hero. He could just about converse in Hindi and had no prior acting experience! Plus, this change of profession was at a time when multiplex cinema had not yet gained credence.

Abraham had a modest start in life. His family of four—father Abraham John, mother Phiruza, his brother Alan and he—lived in Andheri East, a middle-class Mumbai suburb, a far cry from his present upscale sea-facing pad in Bandra Bandstand. Abraham, an economics graduate, earned himself an MBA in marketing from MET Institute and settled into a well-paid job at Enterprise Nexus, an advertising agency. Being a fitness fanatic, he had always worked on his physique. Lady Luck came knocking as he landed a modelling assignment for a denim brand when the designated model didn't turn up on time. He followed it up with a win at Gladrags Manhunt and then there was no looking back. As much a fitness enthusiast then as now, Abraham built on his vital stats and it has all added up pretty well for him.

> I have always been a fighter. And sports people, I realize, are far more gracious losers. They may be defeated but they always fight to win.

After a very successful innings in modelling, Abraham realized that things were beginning to change; a trend of engaging Bollywood stars as brand ambassadors was on the rise. From salt to suits, everybody wanted a film star to endorse their products and Abraham became a casualty of this emerging trend. Though a popular model, he was dropped from the ad campaign of Provogue, a ready-to-wear apparel line. The company favoured Fardeen Khan, a rising film star of the time, over him. Sensing the winds of change, Abraham altered the course of his career once again, and set about exploring the movies option.

The first film that he was signed up for, *Iss Pyaar Ko* by producer–director Rahul Rawail, was shelved. Abraham eventually debuted in *Jism*, which was a huge hit. After the initial success, he tried to choose films that were a good fit for his personality. Some did well while others went unnoticed. But he kept at it till his big chance came with *Dhoom*, which turned his acting career around in a big way.

People often attribute a person's success to being at the right place at the right time, ruing their own fate at not having similar luck. Understanding trends early on is a good way to grab opportunities. Abraham's concerted efforts to keep his ear to the ground and talk to relevant people gives him an edge. Equipped with awareness, he makes sure that he puts his best foot forward and plays to his strengths, making it through every patch, rough or smooth.

PLAY TO WIN

'You were born to win, but to be a winner, you must plan to win, prepare to win, and expect to win.'—ZIG ZIGLAR

A lot of Abraham's memories date back to his schooldays in Bombay Scottish School. He was among the top fifteen in academics but when it came to sports, he was an all-rounder—captain of the soccer team and good at pretty much everything else. According to him, the best thing about his school was that it fostered and encouraged equality among students—a great virtue when you have the crème de la crème of the city sending their children there (Hrithik Roshan, Aditya Chopra, Ekta Kapoor and Ranbir Kapoor, among other VIP kids, studied in Bombay Scottish).

'All class differences would arise only when you stepped out. I travelled in a bus while there were kids who came in gleaming cars,' he recounts without any trace of bitterness.

Well, perhaps that is true of his journey down the Bollywood path as well. What has helped Abraham stay on top of his game is that he plays to win, regardless of whether he gets a level playing field or not. Though he lacks the advantage of belonging to a premier-league showbiz family—a definite plus in the industry—the star has never given that as the reason for the failure of his early films. Instead, he set about understanding the business of cinema and what it takes to remain a star. To his credit he has, over a period of time, worked with the most illustrious and powerful persons in the industry, including the Bhatts (who launched him) the Chopras, the Bachchans, Ekta Kapoor and Karan Johar.

When asked whether being an outsider in the industry was a problem, he concurred, but followed it up with a firm assurance that even though a few contemporaries had the advantage of having roots in the film industry, he would never play the outsider card. 'It's a competitive space and I enjoy it. After all, I am a sportsman. I have always been a fighter. And sportspeople, I realize, are far more gracious losers. They may be defeated but they always fight to win.

'You never win the silver, you lose the gold!' he explains, flashing those famous dimples.

Becoming a winner is not easy. Sure, everyone has dreams, but only those with a plan can fulfil them. Instead of giving up, Abraham ensures that he takes planned steps for every project he ventures into. Adequate research and planning has helped him sail through the most competitive scenarios, putting him in an enviable position.

ENDEARING HONESTY

'Honesty is the first chapter in the book of wisdom.'
—THOMAS JEFFERSON

Abraham's work record in the industry is of a thorough professional, someone who is honest and easy to work with. When he was setting up his production house, a common acquaintance approached him to produce a film. He evaluated the project and was initially extremely excited, before finally turning around to refuse it. When asked why, he apologized profusely and said that while he liked the script and knew that the film would do well, he had to ensure that his first film production was a guaranteed success in order to establish his production house. He went ahead and chose another film, *Vicky Donor*, as his first production, which went on to be a huge hit, winning awards as well as rewards at the box office.

'My father has always said, be honest and don't cheat anyone. Be a good human being. So people should know and even say behind my back that John Abraham is an honest man. Be it the co-producer or studio heads, I don't abuse my privilege.'

A squeaky-clean reputation goes a long way, especially when setting up a business enterprise as Abraham has—a production house that produces films and television commercials.

> I honestly give myself complete credit for any kind of motivation. No one can motivate me more than myself. Seriously! I actually have conversations with myself. And I never give up. So even if my legs are broken, I still believe I can run. I will never go down.

After a hugely successful first film, two more productions have been pencilled in, besides scores of ad films shot by Indian and international directors under his banner JA Entertainment.

Everyone craves success, but to choose the correct path, even while other lucrative deals might be coming your way, is the mark of a real winner. An honest approach is the best way to create long-lasting work associations and given the new corporate culture in Bollywood, Abraham's insistence on doing it right works completely in his favour.

LIVE LIFE THE RIGHT SIZE

*'I am a man of simple tastes.
I am always satisfied with the best.'*—OSCAR WILDE

Abraham lives in a sea-facing bachelor pad, designed by his father and brother. In keeping with his penchant for mean machines, he is the proud owner of numerous cars, as well as vintage bikes. Yet, he continues to be careful with money. He has never been a fashion and lifestyle victim—a common malaise in showbiz. After all, he has made his fortune only after considerable hard work, good luck and astute planning.

Abraham has fond memories of his childhood in the Andheri East neighbourhood, close to where the Bahaar theatre once stood. It was here that he got a glimpse of the frenzy cinema could generate when *Qayamat Se Qayamat Tak* and *Maine Pyar Kiya* (1989) were released. 'It was a basic, fun-filled childhood, thanks in no small measure to my parents. We did simple, fun things like cycle to Khandala and Lonavala...where we broke open watermelons and dunked our heads in it,' he recalls, adding, 'The way I live is still very basic. My friends are the same—from Bombay Scottish. I can enjoy simple food like tendli and karela but I have become a lot more thoughtful as there's more responsibility. I am cautious about how I handle things around me.'

The cars, he concedes, are something of an indulgence, but he compensates for them by investing in good old-fashioned real estate. 'One should invest in assets and not in liabilities,' he maintains. He is the proud owner of a swanky building that houses his office in Mumbai's upscale Pali Hill besides a home in Bel Air, Los Angeles (Source: *Mumbai Mirror*, 25 November 2012). Money, he says, is not an obsession. Be that as it may, he's ensuring that he has more than enough of it in order to make the choices he likes. Though a former supermodel, Abraham prefers a simple T-shirt and jeans look, changing into conventional suits only on formal occasions or for fashion shows. Instead of the frills, he has kept the focus on maintaining a physique that would look good in pretty much anything!

The tendency to go overboard when money rolls in is hard to control, and most begin to flaunt their wealth on attaining a certain level of prosperity. Enjoying the fruits of one's labour, yet living a life with restraint has kept Abraham's fortunes in good shape.

SELF-MOTIVATION

> *'Positive belief in yourself will give you the energy needed to conquer the world and this belief is the power behind all creation.'*—STEPHEN RICHARDS

A never-say-die spirit has been one of Abraham's success mantras.

'I honestly give myself complete credit for any kind of motivation,' says Abraham. 'No one can motivate me more than myself. Seriously! I actually have conversations with myself. And I never give up. So even if my legs are broken, I still believe I can run. I will never go down. In 2010, three of my movies failed in a row and I was told, "Boss, this is the end. Your obituary is ready. You can't resurrect yourself." I heard them out and then I took eight months off to think things through. At that time I decided to do *Force*. I had faith in the film and knew how I would position myself after that. After the film became successful, I became more confident, more sure.'

As it turned out, the self-motivation talks with himself, in addition to some hard-nosed decisions, worked wonders for him! Over the years, it has set Abraham's career on the right track with a reasonably good success ratio, comparable with the strongest competitors.

The journey of life is smoother when one is prepared to handle oneself during the downs. In Abraham's case, he does not seek encouragement from others. Possessing a high level of self-awareness, he turns to himself for unbiased and good advice. His decisions are his own, thought through, tough and effective, because he does not let other's opinions cloud his judgment. That does not mean he won't go wrong; just that when the tide is against him, he is capable of swimming to get himself out of the situation.

UNCONVENTIONAL CHOICES

'Man cannot discover new oceans unless he has the courage to lose sight of the shore.'—ANDRE GIDE

In so many ways one would describe Abraham as conventional—he adores his parents and is involved in their lives; he is protective of his brother and stands staunchly for old-fashioned values, including being courteous, humble and respectful.

However, in terms of his professional choices, it's the untried and untested that has always worked better. He gave up a career in advertising for one in modelling and when he was in his late twenties, opted for movies—considered a risky career choice. *Jism*, an erotic thriller, was the film that defined his career. *Dhoom*, where he played a biker baddie, put him in the reckoning as a star. And *Vicky Donor*, an unusual story about a sperm donor, raked in healthy box office collections, apart from receiving the National Award for wholesome entertainment!

According to Abraham, 'People come to me not because of the films that have worked but because of the films that have not worked; films like *Water, Kabul Express* (2006), *No Smoking* (2007)...I do not stick to formula.'

Abraham realizes that unconventional ideas need to be supported by pragmatic execution; this is where his MBA training comes in. With a risky idea, he is enterprising enough to opt for a plan with room for a healthy return on investment. 'My business acumen helps too—now that's where I come in to marry content with commerce,' emphasizes the actor. *Vicky Donor* and *Madras Cafe*, two of his most risky experiments, paid off both in terms of profits and popularity among cinegoers, proving his ability to make unconventional choices work.

Art needs commerce to support it. Even the most revolutionary ideas need traditional thinking to help them fly. Abraham knows that taking the road less travelled has its pitfalls. So he has fortified himself with conventional business models to be able to support his flights of fancy.

ENTERPRISE STRATEGY, THE JOHN ABRAHAM WAY

Given that he's still some distance from perfecting his craft, John Abraham's success has befuddled many. However, for someone who dropped out of acting school after just one class, he has done rather well, landing roles with leading banners like Yash Raj Films—*Dhoom, Kabul Express, New York;* Dharma Productions—*Kaal* (2005), *Dostana, Dostana 2* (forthcoming*); Balaji Productions—*Shootout At Wadala;* besides his own productions *Vicky Donor* and *Madras Cafe*. His peers often wonder how he's made it so big. He has based his career on a simple lesson from his business school days—play to your strengths, or your 'unique selling proposition' in management-speak. And build on it. Let us look at some of these strengths:

☆ **Brawn power:** Abraham's strategy is pretty simple—to supplement the core requirements of a star with affiliated activities in order to bolster his position. Realizing that his body beautiful is a major draw (even perfectionist Aamir Khan called it one of the best in the business), he picks films that showcase the brawn quotient to advantage. Action films, or light-hearted films like *Dostana* where his physique is the talking point, have served to catapult him into Bollywood's top league. He is now using his fitness skills and know-how for his new business—JA fitness centres—across metros in India.

---
*At the time of writing

- ☆ **Content is king:** Intelligent enough to understand the law of diminishing returns of overexposure, Abraham wisely alternates between movies that play to the gallery (showcasing his physicality) and those that require smart content—newer, more experimental genres that allow him to learn and grow as an actor. He chooses his projects carefully, alternating between the mainstream multi-starrers and formulaic entertainment such as *Race 2* and mixing it up with the eclectic, experimental stuff of the *No Smoking* variety. This way, he continues to be effective in the commercial space while constantly adding value to his acting repertoire. According to him, 'The kind of films I would like to do will be both entertaining and thought-provoking. JA Entertainment means big ideas.'
- ☆ **Brand value:** Though he gave up modelling years ago, he used his experience and familiarity with members of the advertising fraternity to his advantage by featuring in ads even after embarking on a career in films. This was the exact opposite of what some of his fellow models did; they declined brand endorsements as they feared it would overexpose them, reducing their chance of making it big in Bollywood. And by the time they rose to notable positions in showbiz, the endorsement space had been completely taken over by Bollywood stars. Unlike others, Abraham continued in that area. It continues to fetch him big bucks, and there is always a steady flow of creative ad film-makers who want to make films with him, adding great value to his stardom. Now, he even produces ad films under his company.
- ☆ **Real picture:** Perception may be supreme but Abraham

chooses reality over it. People's perceptions do not concern him too much. 'I got a lot of respect for *Water* from a Mark Wahlberg in Hollywood when he saw it, or from a Steven Spielberg when he saw it, to Charlize Theron, only to come back home and be welcomed by the fact that I was a model! So I don't take opinions here very seriously. I think I am damn good at my job and if I was not, I would not have lasted so long.'

His never-say-die spirit and an ability to bring together production facilities for both advertisements and films have enhanced the investor confidence in him. His star power, business acumen, the ability to get the job done within a specified budget besides a reasonably good judgment of script has resulted in studios and corporate companies investing in his production ventures. Besides, he is the only one among his contemporaries to have created a 360-degree business plan around fitness and sports.

RANBIR RAJ KAPOOR
Maximal Focus

'A dream doesn't become reality through magic;
it takes sweat, determination and hard work.'

—Colin Powell

When he gets the opportunity, Ranbir Kapoor, one of Bollywood's most desirable superstars, likes to read biographies or autobiographies of great personalities from all walks of life, such as Andre Agassi's *Open* or Marlon Brando's *Songs My Mother Taught Me*.

'I would rather read about a person who has done something exceptional than read a work of fiction. This is my connect with [the] reality of real people and their achievements,' says Kapoor.

This detail is an important part of the young actor's brilliance. In Bollywood, where stars vie for the 'good actor' label and vice versa, Kapoor is that rare find who has achieved a happy combination of both rather early in his career. And to think that he almost gave an acting career a miss!

As Kapoor mentioned in a recent interview on thebigindianpicture.com, his earliest memory of a film set was that of the movie *Henna* (1991) in which his father Rishi Kapoor played the lead. Watching the actors repeat their lines and dance moves did not impress the young Ranbir. However, sometime during his school years, he figured that pursuing academics was not his cup of tea. Acting seemed a more suitable option, since it didn't involve studying. He surprised everyone when he passed the school board exams, the first to do so in his family, and settled for a course in acting from The Lee Strasberg Theatre and Film Institute.

The rest is history, and Kapoor Junior's academic record seems irrelevant. His performance as an actor has been superlative—Kapoor's debut act in the film *Saawariya* (2007) was impressive enough for him to receive all the awards for the most promising newcomer that year, despite the film's lacklustre performance at the box office. In the six years that followed, the scenario underwent a complete change. Kapoor is now not only acknowledged as an excellent actor but also an indisputable superstar. Each film of his has turned out better than the one preceding it, catapulting his fame to dizzying levels. It's no surprise that he's on every A-list director's wish list.

To say that Ranbir Kapoor has incredible talent is stating the obvious, but what makes him exceptional is his ability to function way beyond the given brief, and his unbridled ambition to do some great work.

Here's looking at how Kapoor gets his act together, time and again.

FOCUS ON THE JOB AT HAND

'The focus should not be on talking [...] It must be on action.'
—HOWARD BERMAN

Six years into his career, even after his talent has been universally acknowledged and his films are doing well, Kapoor refuses to take his work lightly. Usually young actors, even partially successful ones, begin to focus on the frills—personal publicity, endorsement deals, performances—long before the ink has dried on their first autograph. Not Kapoor, who works hard and remains focused.

'As an actor, I am here for the long run. Too many endorsements bring overexposure and it's hard to remain focused. You should be hard-working, honest and passionate. You also need the family's blessings and good wishes,' says the young superstar.

A week before the Annual Screen Awards (2007–08), I met him in the midst of the shooting of *Bachna Ae Haseeno*

(2008), to invite him for the awards ceremony—he was an undisputed contender for the best debut award that year, given his impressive performance in *Saawariya*. Any other actor would have been jumping with joy, eager to soak in his first moments of glory; instead, Kapoor sincerely told me that while he would have loved to be present for the function, it would be unfair to tear himself away from a shoot in progress!

I was rather impressed by his commitment and eagerness to give complete attention to the task at hand. It is unusual in someone that young (he must have been twenty-five at that time). That was just a glimpse of what was to come. In the following years, the young Kapoor scion impressed everyone with his bravura performances in roles as varied as chalk and cheese. The young actor did not seem to be in any hurry to sign films or perform at live events or even sign up endorsements, unlike several from his ilk.

'With endorsements, there is a lot of exposure and it becomes hard to focus. PR exercises spell the death of an actor. One knows of actors trying to put out news about themselves [outside of films]. When you start doing that, you lose steam.' This is something that the young star has always maintained.

When he did start performing at live shows, he remained choosy, refusing to allow big bucks to tempt him into signing too many gigs. And once he made up his mind about it, he signed up for just a single event in a year. In 2013, when he agreed to perform at the Screen Awards, watching him rehearse his steps the night before was a joy. He worked his way through the elaborate sequence with many changes, rehearsing painstakingly to get it right. On the awards night, he had a minor wardrobe malfunction—his clown's nose fell off! It was at the end of his act, which was loved by the crowds. Any other actor would have simply asked for that part to be edited, but Kapoor stayed back after the show to re-enact that part, so that it was set right for the TV recording of the show.

Getting the job done is one thing, but getting it done perfectly requires focus. Often it needs repetition, which can be a tad weary. But in doing so diligently, one hones one's skills, and over time perfection becomes second nature. Kapoor's willingness to pass up the glamorous activities and stay the course ensures him top billing among his contemporaries.

DON'T REST ON YOUR LAURELS

'Nothing wilts faster than laurels that have been rested upon.'
—PERCY BYSSHE SHELLEY

Kapoor had the most opulent debut that any newcomer could have wished for. *Saawariya* was a big-ticket film with a lavish budget, helmed by Sanjay Leela Bhansali, the maker of larger-than-life movies such as *Hum Dil De Chuke Sanam* (1999), *Devdas* (2002) and *Black* (2005). The industry was agog with curiosity about the newcomers in that film, Ranbir Kapoor and Sonam Kapoor. However, the melancholic story, despite its poetic narration, failed to impress moviegoers, but not before giving the film industry a brand new superstar—Ranbir Raj Kapoor, who danced like a dream, was good-looking, but above all, could act like he was to the camera born!

Kapoor has since followed up his debut with superlative performances in *Bachna Ae Haseeno, Wake up Sid* (2009), *Ajab Prem Ki Ghazab Kahani* (2009), *Rocket Singh: Salesman of the Year* (2009), *Raajneeti*, *RockStar* (2011) and *Barfi!* (2012).

> You want to be the biggest star or the biggest actor. The problem with me is that I want to be both. I want to be the best of everyone.

Superstar Shah Rukh Khan has gone on record to say that he was impressed by how good Kapoor was even at the beginning of his career. Perfectionist Aamir Khan has acknowledged him as one of the finest actors of his generation. But high praise from seniors and contemporaries apart, Kapoor always has an accurate assessment of his own performance, regardless of a film's failure or success. Even though his film *Raajneeti* turned out to be a spectacular success, he was quick to own up to the shortcomings in his performance. 'I think the response that I got for *Raajneeti* was undeserving. I don't think I milked the role as much as I should have. Even if the movie is a success, I can't just sit back and say "job well done". I think I could have contributed more to the character. The film contributed more to me than I could [to it] as an actor!'

Despite the fact that he is an inheritor of the legacy of his grandfather Raj Kapoor's banner RK Films, Kapoor has opted to float his own production house, Picture Shuru Productions, to test his mettle as an actor–producer.

No one can achieve perfection in one fell stroke. More often than not, it is a process, not an event and therefore, moving on from one's earlier achievements and glory is crucial. Kapoor's ability to constantly look ahead has kept him from allowing complacence to set in, propelling him into the big league.

DO YOUR HOMEWORK

*'For every two minutes of glamour,
there are eight hours of hard work.'*—JESSICA AVITCH

That Kapoor was no flash in the pan was clear by the time he appeared in his second film, *Bachna Ae Haseeno*. By the third, *Ajab Prem Ki Ghazab Kahani*, the industry and the audience were more than convinced of his exceptional talent. Given his lineage—he belongs to a legendary Bollywood family with four generations of actors—one may think that success came to him on a platter. Such an assumption, though natural, is not entirely true. What his starry lineage assured him was access and a natural curiosity from the audience. The success and popularity that followed was destiny by design.

The young actor, though capable of bagging a good project based solely on his exalted lineage, chose to study acting in New York University and The Lee Strasberg Theatre and Film Institute. He then decided to work with Sanjay Leela Bhansali as an assistant director before embarking on his journey as an actor. In that capacity, he helped train child actor Ayesha

---

If you start taking your work for granted, all the attention will go away. I don't want to do dishonest work. I come from a certain family but I don't want to rest on their laurels. I want to make a name for my own self. I want my father to be known as Ranbir Kapoor's father. Achievement to me is being happy and proud of the work that you do. Also, to bring a smile on my parents' face.

Kapoor for her award-winning performance as a deaf-mute in the movie *Black*. He even acted in a short film *India, 1964* (2004) directed by Abhay Chopra (film-maker B.R. Chopra's grandson). The short film was nominated for a Student Oscar. Before starting work on *Saawariya*, he analysed Hindi movies from the 1940s till 2007, in order to understand the nuances of different styles of film-making and acting in Hindi cinema. His logic was simple—to be a part of Bollywood, a thorough understanding of Hindi cinema was a must. Merely watching Western films, he realized, would not do the trick.

It is admirable that he does not take his star status or his lineage for granted. His mentor from the early days, film-maker Sanjay Leela Bhansali, has always spoken highly of Kapoor's commitment to the craft. According to Bhansali, Kapoor is full of beans and extremely clued in about all the industry goings-on too! But once on the set he is disciplined, hard-working and completely dedicated, with unwavering focus.

When shooting for a film, Kapoor prefers to hang out with the team, including the director, writers and set designers, to help him understand his character better, instead of isolating himself in his vanity van. His modus operandi is simple enough—to absorb from the people who envisage and imagine a scene long before the actor comes into the picture. Being with them helps him understand the character better. 'I have grown up with film directors and music directors around me. I am a student of cinema. My learning curve is subconscious. I think I am becoming more ambitious everyday but there is no plan,' sums up Kapoor.

Making sure that every facet of one's task is understood before one embarks on it is by far the best way to achieve success. This involves delving into areas that may seem unrelated or perhaps only remotely connected, but then perfection lies in covering the details.

DETACHED DISTANCE

*'By letting it go, it all gets done.
The world is won by those who let it go.'*—LAO TZU

Regardless of success or failure, life goes on. But as we know, insecurity is a common sentiment among professional rivals and given the competitive nature of the film industry, it is even greater there. However, Kapoor's attitude of not following the herd mentality when it comes to choosing projects and endorsements is indeed admirable. As an actor, he treats the script like a Bible. Regardless of the choices made by his contemporaries, Kapoor has picked the most unconventional scripts, even those that his father, veteran actor Rishi Kapoor, deemed risky. Such as *Barfi!*, the love story of a deaf-mute boy and an autistic girl.

I asked him once, in an interview, about his approach and whether he was influenced in any way by competition in general. Did he ever feel the need to follow what his contemporaries like Imran Khan or Shahid Kapoor, or his seniors, were doing? He replied, 'I don't think of success or failure [of the film] too much. You have to do what keeps you happy. You cannot be too self-assured or paranoid. It has to be a bit of both. You have to be real and work hard. If my

> If there is one thing and the only thing that I am arrogant about, it's my talent. But for being the biggest star, I still have to cover some distance.

movies don't do well then I need to stop, take a reality check and introspect.' This unhurried and calm detachment about work is a rare quality, especially in one so young.

The oft-heard line 'He/she lives and breathes his work' is often misleading. The truly involved person calmly assesses the task at hand, prepares for it and then goes about it.

AMBITIOUS AND MORE

'Intelligence without ambition is a bird without wings.'
—SALVADOR DALI

Kapoor has set high standards for himself. Among his favourite anecdotes about stardom is one about his grandfather, actor Raj Kapoor's visit to Russia for the premiere of his film *Shree 420* (1955). Kapoor Senior was aware that his films were popular in Russia, but when he stepped out of the screening, his Russian fans who had gathered outside carried his car to the hotel! That madness, according to the younger Kapoor, defines stardom in the real sense, the kind he would like to create for himself. He is already working on it, mixing up a heady cocktail with his choice of films—urbane, such as *Wake Up Sid*, meant for a more select audience, as well as films that cater to a larger audience like *Yeh Jawaani Hai Deewani* (2013), *Ajab Prem Ki Ghazab Kahaani*, *Barfi!* and *Besharam* (2013). He has upped the ante further by turning producer, along with director Anurag Basu, for *Jagga Jasoos* (forthcoming[*]), a fun detective caper, the first of his contemporaries to take the leap. 'You want to be the biggest star or the biggest actor.

---
[*]At the time of writing

The problem with me is that I want to be both. I want to be the best of everyone because there's so much to emulate from superstars but you can't really follow anyone's path. Everyone's journey is different, though your goals can be similar,' says Bollywood's new favourite.

Ambition is often looked upon negatively. Perhaps because it is assumed that one needs to trample on others in the race to get ahead. Often, it does amount to such. But true ambition is an attempt to carve a distinct identity for oneself, so distinct that it totally redefines an individual's perception. Kapoor has managed to achieve this within a very short span of time.

DON'T TAKE IT EASY

'You never can take for granted that you have a job.'
—BENJAMIN WALKER

By the time Kapoor started work on *RockStar*, he was already part of the big league. Being the most sought-after star, he could afford to throw starry tantrums, report late on the film sets or not land up at all.

He did nothing of the sort. Instead, he hung out with the film's director Imtiaz Ali and the rest of the team in order to cull information about the role he had to play, of Janardhan aka Jordan, the Jat boy who wants to become a famous musician. He even spent time with a Jat family and went shopping with them for the jeans he wore in the film, all as part of understanding the character.

According to Kapoor, 'If you start taking your work for granted, all the attention will go away. I don't want to do dishonest work. I come from a certain family but I don't want to rest on their laurels. I want to make a name for my own self. I want my father to be known as Ranbir Kapoor's father. Achievement to me is being happy and proud of the work that you do. Also, to bring a smile on my parents' face.'

To assume that super-success cannot be bettered is a fallacy. Even impossible world records have been broken after years of staying untouched. The man who tries to break his own record constantly sets new standards with every fresh attempt.

REALITY CHECK

'There is a fine line between dreams and reality, it's up to you to draw it.'—B. QUILLIAM

As a young boy who grew up in a protected environment, Kapoor realized early on in life that he needed more exposure. After an unremarkable stint in Bombay Scottish School and HR College, he set sail for the US, where he spent three and a half years away from his family and trained in acting, something that no one else from the Kapoor clan had done! To them, acting came naturally.

All he had to do was to ask his father to launch him in a film (a tradition that was adopted by numerous family members). But Kapoor had cleared the cobwebs in his head and decided to pursue an acting career seriously; yet, he wanted to be sure that even if he failed as an actor, his background and training in the subject would ensure him a decent livelihood.

This seemingly insignificant detail of the actor's life is pertinent, as it points to the strong reality check he has in place. He understands the importance of focusing on the core job, rather than concentrating on the frills.

In fact, Kapoor is among the few actors who keeps a low profile, surfacing only when there is a film coming up for release.

Highly conscious of his strengths and weaknesses, Kapoor has always been self-assured about his acting skills. Yet, interestingly, he has not lost sight of the fact that he still has some way to go before he becomes a huge star. Despite his success in a variety of roles, he picks his projects carefully, aware that younger, boyish characters like the ones in *Wake Up Sid* or *Barfi!* are better fits for him than, say, a Chulbul Pandey in *Dabangg* (2010). It was only after two major hits, *Barfi!* and *Yeh Jawaani Hai Deewani*, that he attempted *Besharam*, a massy entertainer, which was a departure from his earlier films. The gamble did not pay off, a fact that he duly acknowledged. Of course, he's very confident that he will get there sooner than later.

'If there is one thing and the only thing that I am arrogant about, it's my talent. But for being the biggest star, I still have to cover some distance,' is Kapoor's modest contention.

To know one's strengths and weaknesses requires an enormous amount of self-assessment. Most people are wary of doing so because they feel that they might find flaws that they cannot surmount. But confronting one's shortcomings fully prepares one for the steps needed when the going gets tough. It is actually an asset.

TRULY, MADLY, DEEPLY: RANBIR KAPOOR STYLE

Kapoor may be in the news as much for matters of the heart as his trail-blazing career, but there is never a murmur of discontent from those that he works for. In fact, A-list directors such as Anurag Basu, Anurag Kashyap and Imtiaz Ali are all part of his inner circle and continue to team up with him. He was perhaps the first actor in recent times to agree to work with ex-girlfriend Deepika Padukone in *Yeh Jawaani Hai Deewani,* in the larger interest of the film. The secret to Kapoor's popularity lies in an amazing skill set and an unparalleled ability to lift a film from mediocre to superlative with his powerhouse performances. Here's a lowdown on how to make it happen, Ranbir style:

☆ **De-glam duties:** Being part of a profession just because your friends are in it or to fulfil your parents' dream or because it is glamorous could end up rather badly. Kapoor chose his job wisely though. He did not get into films because three generations of his family were part of them. After some trial and error, he figured that he would be far happier dabbling in acting or something film-related, rather than being part of a multinational corporation. He tested waters by first enrolling for an acting course and then working as an assistant director before finally taking the plunge. Besides, the young actor is perfectly happy working on the non-glamorous aspects of film-making, which gives him an edge over those who can't think beyond eight packs and a new hairstyle.

☆ **Security blanket:** One of the most significant aspects to contribute to Kapoor's rise is that he is secure in his own space. He does compare and compete with the best in business, but he also displays a clear and surefooted understanding of his own place in the food chain vis-à-vis his seniors and juniors.

He may have updates on what others are doing, but his agenda is not really set by their itinerary. At a time when contemporaries and juniors were falling over each other to perform at award functions and live shows, he held back till he was satisfied with his repertoire of songs. Waiting for the opportune moment worked in his favour. It enhanced his exclusivity, lending him a premium price tag.

☆ **Long-term view:** An ability to plan beyond the immediate is intrinsically linked to being secure. An awareness that he is in the movies for the long haul keeps Kapoor from knee-jerk reactions in his choice of films or endorsements. The choice of his films varies from eclectic to masala, regardless of box office prospects.

☆ **Confidence in talent:** Though extremely proud of his lineage, Kapoor is aware that it can only take him so far. Talent, he realizes, is a better investment in a creative industry like the movies. The Kapoor family name burns bright because of their contribution to cinema and he hopes to continue with the fine tradition. With his impressive roles in movies like *RockStar, Rocket Singh:*

> *Salesman of the Year, Barfi!* and *Raajneeti*, the young actor has also generated tremendous confidence among filmmakers. At present, he is among a few premium stars who are signed up for projects regardless of the fate of their previous films.

AISHWARYA RAI BACHCHAN
Grace under Pressure

'Grace in women has more effect than beauty.'
—WILLIAM HAZLITT

Her name is often prefixed with achievements—former Miss World, Padma Shri, Bollywood actor, brand ambassador, United Nations' Goodwill Ambassador for creating awareness about HIV/AIDS, as well as UN spokesperson for microcredit finance, among others. The most significant designation, though, by her own admission, was acquired when she became mom to daughter Aaradhya.

Aishwarya Rai Bachchan's glamorous and notable résumé does make a lasting impression, but the qualities that separate her from the crowd are her grace and dignity and the ability to be on top of her game in the face of the most extreme criticism. She always remains unruffled, displaying a calm front under the most trying circumstances that could make the toughest of people have a meltdown. This has ensured the actress the numero uno position, despite the highs and lows in both her personal and professional life.

While the milestones of Rai's life have been widely chronicled and celebrated, her impressive journey from a middle-class Mumbai–Mangalorean girl to India's most celebrated glamour icon would be incomplete without tracing her remarkable composure and manoeuvring of downturns and upswings in her eventful journey. Being criticized for her sartorial sense, dropped from a prestigious film for demanding a higher remuneration, being ousted from projects on account of a turbulent personal relationship—no matter how despairing the lows may have been, Rai has come out of it triumphant. Here's how she achieves it, time and again.

COUNT YOUR BLESSINGS

'If you come to fame not understanding who you are, it will define who you are.'—OPRAH WINFREY

'You would be a fool to deny the obvious when you choose the world of glamour and movies as a career option. Indian cinema has the kind of impact. Once you make this choice, scrutiny will go with the territory. When it is fictitious or just partially true, I am human enough to get frustrated or hurt because I am extremely sensitive in nature [sic]. All creative people are, irrespective of what they show the world.

'It is important to remember when times are tough [to] focus on the amount of good there is. When you focus on that [the good], it reveals that negativity is a much smaller entity. It becomes easier to overcome uncomfortable situation[s],' says Rai of her ability to squarely face hardships that come her way.

This lesson of acceptance and preservation of the good in one's life was something that she learnt early in life. Particularly insightful is an interview to Rediff wherein she recounted, 'There was this "good girl", this "achiever" kind of aura around me. I am not saying I was egoistic, but there was a certain level of confidence. My parents never pushed me but it was taken for granted because I came first. When I came to the tenth grade, my seniors and juniors, everybody thought I'd top the ICSE Board exams. But I came seventh or eighth in class. That was a huge blow. That's when it hurt because I had not valued my first rank until then. That was the only time I cried.'

Rai went on to finish Class 12 from Ruparel College and pursue a degree in architecture. Fortunately for her, her parents and people around her had a balanced viewpoint. 'I have always had this middle-of-the-road perspective since the 12th standard. I never got swept away by success or bogged down by failure.'

When she came second in the Miss India beauty pageant, Rai refused to be disheartened, firm in the belief that the outcome, not matter what her position, was the same—she would be going for an international pageant, only Miss World instead of Miss Universe. As it transpired, she won the Miss World title and went on to become a top-notch star with global footprints. Her ability to focus on the good and move on to the next challenge has ensured her a place among the best in the business.

Besides, the actress has always maintained that God has blessed her with plenty and she is always thankful for the good around her. She mentions her special relationship with God in many interviews and conversations, and in difficult times too, never loses sight of the fact that her life is indeed a blessed one. A regular at Mumbai's Siddhivinayak temple, the prayers she offers are always full of gratitude.

> Post the titles [Miss World] I was virtually like the Indian representative. People have given me that kind of place and love so there is no question of feeling the need to move away. It perhaps made me more rooted. Or probably made me recognize being Indian that much more, early in my life.

It is a fool who squanders away the blessings bestowed upon him, while a wise person nurtures them. Only those who understand this adage reach their maximum potential. Rai's early discernment of this philosophy has helped her leverage her strengths—matchless beauty and innate grace—to the best possible advantage.

LOOK BEFORE YOU LEAP

'The enlightened ruler is heedful, and the good general full of caution.'—SUN TZU

When a turbulent personal relationship led to her being ousted from some very prestigious films, Rai refused to overreact or indulge in a blame game. Despite the perception that being dropped from such A-list films could have a detrimental effect on her career, she did not court the media in order to give 'her side of the story' or to take up cudgels against her detractors.

Instead, she lay low and put her house in order. First, she issued a press release informing the media and public at large that she had moved on from the said relationship. The announcement put an end to speculations about her personal life and brought the focus firmly on the positive developments in her career, which, with the runaway success of *Devdas*, was on an upswing.

Instead of reacting to her name being struck off these prestigious projects, in 2003 she signed up for *Chokher Bali* (2003) directed by Rituparno Ghosh, and produced *Dil Ka Rishta* (2003) with her brother Aditya, scripted by her mother Vrinda Rai. Despite the fact that it was not a hit, the latter move worked in her favour, establishing her as an actress with her own clout, as no heroine of her generation could boast of pulling off a home production entirely on personal steam.

Actions speak louder than words. Many a time, one believes that one can make an impact just by talking big. But it is only doing the right things that makes a lasting impression and earns the respect of others. Rai's actions reflected a positive and forward-looking attitude that made others forget the past and admire her strengths.

MIX MODERNITY AND CONVENTION

'You don't really need modernity in order to exist totally and fully. You need a mixture of modernity and tradition.'
—THEODORE BIKEL

At father-in-law Amitabh Bachchan's seventieth birthday celebration, Rai was seen standing along with hubby Abhishek Bachchan to greet the guests, but between her responsibilities as the daughter-in-law, she would intermittently disappear to check on her daughter Aaradhya. In that moment, seeing her involved in family matters like any other woman, one could have easily forgotten that she was a former Miss World, an international celebrity!

Though it shocked Oprah Winfrey that Abhishek Bachchan and Aishwarya Rai lived in a joint family with parents, Rai made the transition to being the daughter-in-law of Bollywood's first family seem like a cakewalk. She took to her new responsibilities rather well, always maintaining that it had been easy, as she was accustomed to living in a joint family. The only change she made was to leave the sets immediately after pack up. 'Our jobs demand us to travel constantly and squeezing in that family time together becomes crucial,' said Rai in an interview for *Screen*. After the arrival of

> I am grateful for the opportunities that came my way. So the interest came from there [Hollywood] and for me it was always [about] striking a balance.

daughter Aaradhya, she devoted the last couple of years to being the perfect mommy, even during her visit to Cannes or while travelling around the country for various endorsements.

Rai's public conduct has always been guided by an acknowledgement of her position as one of India's representatives to the world. The genesis of her penchant for playing a cultural ambassador lies in her being selected as the country's representative at the Miss World pageant. 'I was very clear that everything Indian was very ingrained in me. As a model I was seen as a people's person, and not as a regular model. Post the titles [Miss World] I was virtually like the Indian representative. People have given me that kind of place and love so there is no question of feeling the need to move away. It perhaps made me more rooted. Or probably made me recognize being Indian that much more, early in my life.'

However, the remarkable thing about Rai is that while she has never strayed from convention, she has lived by her own rules, never allowing the pursuit of fame to become the fulcrum of her existence.

Unlike most aspiring actresses, Rai was never a keen advocate of showing skin or doing intimate scenes, unless it was a necessity. She changed her policy on lip locks (in *Dhoom 2*) only after such scenes had gained greater acceptance in Hindi films. And for much of her international career, she remained the Indian girl who did not succumb to the Western standards of exposure and intimacy.

'I just conduct myself the way I have been brought up to conduct myself; to give my best to whatever I do with complete conviction,' she says.

Knowing how to balance tradition and modernity is an exercise in itself. The push and pull of modern living has created a situation where coexistence of the two is difficult. Rai's deft handling of each situation according to its demand and her inherent ability to draw the line where required has helped her traverse Bollywood's tricky terrain rather well.

RECOGNIZE YOUR OWN POTENTIAL

'With realization of one's own potential and self-confidence in one's own ability, one can build a better world.'—DALAI LAMA XIV

An incredibly bright student who achieved top grades through school and college, Rai could have pursued a career in architecture but she chose to drop out of academics to take up modelling. Her good looks and charisma made her an instant success, and pretty soon she had established herself as a top-rung model.

It was around this time that she began getting offers from Bollywood. However, instead of jumping on to the Bollywood bandwagon—even though she had received offers from A-league film-makers like Yash Chopra—she bided her time and focused her attention on the Miss India pageant. Unlike others who take to modelling and films after they win pageants, Rai was already a top model at the time she decided to take part in a beauty contest. She ran the risk of not winning and becoming the laughing stock of the modelling fraternity. As luck would have it, she did not win the top crown at Miss India, but she took it on the chin to prepare for what lay ahead—the Miss World competition. Every move of hers had been under tremendous scrutiny because Sushmita Sen, the winner of Miss India, had already bagged the Miss Universe title. It was under intense pressure that she competed in the Miss World pageant.

However, she sailed through, and the rest is history.

'Dream, have your aspirations but it is important to recognize your own potential. I remember in my student life I was a topper throughout school and who would have thought I would be the dropout from college! It's not something that I am proud of, but in retrospect, I am glad of the course my life took,' is Rai's take on being courageous enough to dream big.

Taking the unpredictable route instead of the tried and tested one can be scary. But it is in these choices that one's confidence and assessment of one's potential is tested. Why settle for mere baubles, when one can reach for the stars? Rai, sure of her own competence, has always seized opportunities that have come her way, even when doing so meant working extra hard.

BRANCHING OUT SHALL BEAR FRUIT

'Career diversification ain't a bad thing.'—VIN DIESEL

Rai surprised everyone by attempting regional cinema (Tamil), before giving in to the call of Bollywood. She refused films such as *Raja Hindustani* (1996), *Kuch Kuch Hota Hai* (1998) and *Hum Saath Saath Hain* (1999), choosing to flag off her career with Mani Ratnam's *Iruvar* (1997) instead! Though the film, also starring Mohanlal, was not commercially successful, Rai found plenty of takers in the Hindi film industry. *Aur Pyaar Ho Gaya* (1997) was her first Bollywood movie, followed by *Aa Ab Laut Chalein* (1997), directed by Rishi Kapoor. Over time, she built her Bollywood repertoire with hits such as *Taal* (1999), *Josh* (2000), *Hum Dil De Chuke Sanam*, *Devdas* and *Mohabattein* (2000).

On receiving international film offers, Rai decided it was time to strike out beyond Bollywood. In a short span, she became India's unofficial brand ambassador in Hollywood; several Indian actors have had their cover moment on *Time*, but Rai is likely to be the only one to have been on the cover as one of the hundred most influential people in the world, besides being invited on respected and widely followed American shows like *60 Minutes, The David Letterman Show* and *The Oprah Winfrey Show*.

Rai has always played her cards intelligently—by criss-crossing regional cinema and making her debut opposite a stalwart like Mohanlal, she tried out her acting chops without the pressures of stardom that would have accompanied a Bollywood film. Besides the exposure of working with a great director and a seasoned actor, she also strengthened her fan following before embarking on a career in Hindi films. Even today, she remains a favourite choice for big-ticket Southern movies, for instance, *Enthiran (The Robot)* (2010).

According to Rai, 'I am grateful for the opportunities that came my way. So the interest came from there (Hollywood) and for me it was always [about] striking a balance.'

More often than not, people strive for expertise in a single arena, assuming it to be a sure-fire way to succeed. But as a famous man said, 'Specialization is for insects.' By choosing to work in different regions and with different sets of people, Rai opened herself up to new experiences, resulting in a truly holistic understanding of the profession that she is in. Branching out, in her case, paved the way to global stardom, putting her in a different league altogether.

WALK THE TALK

'It isn't what you have or who you are or where you are or what you are doing that makes you happy or unhappy. It is what you think about it.'—DALE CARNEGIE

Almost all beauty queens talk about inner beauty or how they will embrace the vicissitudes of age. But truth is that at the first given opportunity, they go under the knife for the perfect nose or for slicing off the unwanted pounds on their body beautiful. Not Rai! She has shown herself to be a woman of her words. When vitriolic criticism greeted her red carpet appearance with her post-pregnancy pounds at the Festival de Cannes in 2012, the former Miss World simply put her best foot forward, and faced the flashbulbs with a winsome smile. And with that singular action, she asserted that it was all right for women to be their natural selves, a few inches here or there notwithstanding.

Critics were unsparing, pointing out that Rai's position as a beauty queen made it her singular duty to dazzle at such events with a perfectly sculpted figure at all times, but Rai just went about her duties as a brand ambassador, never once demurring from her work and abiding by the principles she lives by.

Earlier, on being asked about the criticism

> One has to give completely to receive in abundance. Oprah is an inspiration in terms of making a difference to people's lives. There have been baby steps but I think it's very, very important to impact larger multitudes of lives. I would feel wasted if I did not do my bit socially.

she received almost every year for her red carpet appearances (once she was even compared to a dowager sofa set), she asserted, 'Being well turned out and aptly dressed for occasions is important, but at the same time it's important to not be obsessive about it because it is a whirlpool. It can get you sucked in and take focus away from what really matters in life.'

As naysayers cried themselves hoarse about her appearance, she made headlines in the international press by drawing attention to India's newfound obsession, an unhealthy one at that, with unreal vital stats. She also made it to the World's Most Beautiful Women list in *New York* magazine, 2012, proving that conviction and confidence are the best things you can wear on your sleeve!

The pressure to conform is the foremost reason for people losing their individuality. As one goes through life, it is important to decide what one stands for and move ahead accordingly—even if it means facing the wrath or ridicule of short-sighted critics. Ultimately people come around, but only when one displays courage and conviction consistently. Rai definitely sets an example.

DON'T GIVE IN TO PRESSURE

'No pressure. No diamonds.'—THOMAS CARLYLE

Rai, always aware of her advantageous position in the grand scheme of things, has never ever allowed herself to be short-changed professionally. Even though she had no prior experience or background in the business side of showbiz, the actress used her education well, negotiating her own deals and contracts, pretending that she had a lawyer who was putting down the terms and conditions! She recalls the gimmick with both humility and amusement, thankful that seniors in the industry indulged her and went along with the charade. Adman Prahlad Kakkar, who has known her since the time she appeared in her first ad for Pepsi, has always maintained that she is truly a beauty with brains. This smartness was most evident at the time she signed up for film-maker Ketan Mehta's *Mangal Pandey: The Rising* (2005). Around the same time, a leading Hollywood agency had stepped in to manage her affairs, pitching the actress as a new talent in Hollywood.

According to reports, since *Mangal Pandey: The Rising* was slated for an international release, with an English version along with the Hindi one, the agency had suggested that Rai be paid a corrective price (at par with a remuneration that suited her positioning as an international talent), which at that time was unheard of for an actress. Rai was dropped from the project by producer Bobby Bedi for demanding a paycheck equal to that of a Bollywood hero, but she refused to compromise on her stand. In a male-dominated film industry, a lesser person would have crumbled or launched into a series of explanations, but she did nothing of the sort. She just continued with the unflinching detachment of a Zen master and set about her international career, having signed up for foreign-based projects such as *Bride & Prejudice* (2004), *Mistress of Spices* (2005), *Provoked* (2006), *The Last Legion* (2007) and *The Pink Panther 2* (2009). And if that wasn't impressive enough, Rai was invited to the Festival de Cannes as one of the jury members too.

'Give your best to what you do and don't give in to pressure' is the motto she has consistently maintained throughout her career.

People will always try to push you into a place that is

advantageous to themselves. More often than not, one tends to take the line of least resistance to go with the flow. Sometimes, to achieve a higher objective, one has to take a stand that could translate into a short-term disadvantage. Rai has always stood her ground and turned adverse situations to her advantage.

BEAUTY IS AS BEAUTY DOES

'A mode of conduct, a standard of courage, discipline, fortitude and integrity can do a great deal to make a woman beautiful.'
—JACQUELINE BISSET

Long ago, I had an unexpected brush with Rai at Mount Mary Basilica in Bandra, Mumbai. She was accompanying a friend who wanted to offer prayers at the altar. Knowing that her presence could disturb others at the church, she stood quietly in one corner patiently waiting for her friend to finish with the proceedings before they made their way out. Her consideration for others is something that has often been endorsed by those who have interacted with her. Among her ardent supporters are Simi Garewal, former leading actress and renowned television anchor, and leading author–columnist Shobhaa De. Directors Sanjay Leela Bhansali and Ashutosh Gowariker, whom she has worked with, have often described her as a thorough professional, extremely hard-working, besides being a wonderful person.

Rai carries her graciousness beyond her close circle of friends and professional associates. Soon after she became Miss World, she pledged her eyes for donation to a Mumbai-based NGO. It was a wonderful gesture from someone whose eyes are considered her most alluring feature. It was a hint of things to come. Since then, she has been involved with various charities, the most recent being signing up as the United Nations' Goodwill Ambassador for AIDS awareness.

'One has to give completely to receive in abundance. Oprah is an inspiration in terms of making a difference to people's lives. There have been baby steps but I think it's very, very important to impact larger multitudes of lives. I would feel wasted if I did not do my bit socially,' maintains the actress.

What good is the power and fame that one acquires, if it cannot help those in need? Rai has put her fame to good use, channeling it to help those who are at a disadvantage. She well and truly practises this philosophy and sincerely believes that little by little, she can effect great change using the position that has been acquired by her.

AISHWARYA'S WINNING WAYS

Being exquisitely beautiful and accepted universally for it can be extremely tough, and Rai is no exception. For every plaudit that she receives, there is an equal amount of criticism. More often than not, critics wave her off as an average actor but instead of lashing out at detractors, she silently proved them wrong with her achievements. Despite the highs and lows in her life, she continues to get top billing, be it endorsements or film projects, and one of the major reasons for this is her ability to steer clear of acrimonious exchanges. For her part, the actress has never allowed herself to have a public meltdown, so common to celebrities who lead fishbowl lives. She has just moved from one achievement to another.

☆ **Positive plus:** Aishwarya Rai Bachchan's ability to focus on the positives of her spectacular career has held her in good stead. Unlike several contemporaries, she has held her own even in competitive spaces, without resorting to desperate measures to further her career. It has been one of the reasons for her rise to the numero uno position.

☆ **Avoid public displays:** Several people may consider keeping a lid on one's emotions stifling but in the long run, a squeaky-clean attitude helps. Thanks to her positive image, Rai has been the face of cosmetic giant L'Oreal for eleven years. She may have had her share of controversies, but her ability to hold her peace and put forward a measured response to get across her side of the story has always held her in good stead.

☆ **Pressure resistant:** The life of a film celebrity, though charmed, is never easy and pressure from all quarters on how they should behave, things they should say, movies they should act in or how they should look, is tremendous. The trick is to avoid the pitfalls it brings, something Rai has mastered. She does not allow unnecessary pressure to force her hand. She keeps counsel and leads her life as per her beliefs, and not according to others' expectations of her as a celebrity.

☆ **Traditionally modern:** There is no shame in being traditional. Rai's conventional family approach—she has, for most of her life, lived in a joint family—may befuddle Oprah Wintrey but within India it has earned her more admirers than one can count. Equally, her ability to pull off a modern and glamorous avatar year after year at Cannes and several international appearances such as at the Academy Awards, Oprah Winfrey's show and so on, has earned her admirers around the world. Everyone from Will Smith to Julia Roberts to Hugh Jackman speaks highly of Aishwarya Rai Bachchan as the most beautiful woman in the world.

HRITHIK ROSHAN
Overcoming the Achilles' Heel

'Obstacles don't have to stop you. If you run into a wall, don't turn around and give up. Figure out how to climb it, go through it or walk around it.'

—MICHAEL JORDAN

As Hrithik Roshan's name blazoned across the cinema screens in *Kaho Naa...Pyaar Hai* (2000), there was no doubt in anyone's mind that a new superstar had arrived. The hysteria around him was a phenomenon in itself. But the most remarkable feat in Roshan's march to superstardom was his personal triumph against a handicap that could hamstring any actor's progress.

The actor's impressive strides in showbiz since his debut in 2000—films that range in theme from action to historical and superhero, a clutch of brand endorsements, television shows and live performances around the world—have placed him among Bollywood's much coveted, top-rung stars. Roshan is counted among the most versatile actors, one of the few male stars from Bollywood being considered by Hollywood studios for a possible crossover film. Better known as Bollywood's very own Greek God, Roshan regularly features on lists of the sexiest and most beautiful people in India.

In the glitter and gleam of his glamorous life, it would be easy to imagine that all this was handed to him on a platter. The truth, however, is a little different. Around the age of six, Duggu (as Roshan is fondly called by his parents and friends), developed a speech problem. He began to stammer, a development which, according to him, was nothing short of a living nightmare. In a bid to overcome this problem he underwent years of

> Maybe I have so many faults that people who watch me spend time rectifying them think I am perfecting my shots. I have deep passion for my work and a lot of broken tools that I employ. I need to spend more time for each film which is why I can't do ten films a year.

speech therapy and rehearsals, which helped him coordinate his breath, lips and internal muscles till he was on top of his game. And finally, in 2000, when he made a spectacular debut, everyone just sat back and stared in wonder.

The same determination surfaced when Roshan suffered severe back and knee injuries. However, he bounced back resolutely with *Kites* (2010) and *Agneepath* that had high-wattage action and soon started planning *Krrish 3*, part of his superhero movie series. In 2013, he developed a clot in his brain because of performing certain daredevil stunts. The clot was removed surgically, resulting in a short embargo on the actor's action sequences but he was back within a week, enthusiastically promoting *Krrish 3* and planning a surprise birthday party for his father. *Krrish 3* went on to become one of his biggest hits, earning over ₹200 crore.

To have gone through these impediments and yet pulled off a superlative career in the movies that requires dialogue delivery, dancing and emoting before a crew of a hundred or more people, not to mention the millions who watch the film, is indeed a heroic achievement.

Here's looking at Roshan's secret ways of conquering fears and going from hero to superhero.

EFFORTS UNLIMITED

'Strength doesn't come from what you can do. It comes from overcoming the things you once thought you couldn't.'
—*ANONYMOUS*

Roshan has never fought shy of speaking about his speech problems, which started when he was six years old. He has shared his example on several occasions to inspire others. 'Everything seems normal till you start talking. The minute you start talking, you get stuck and you don't know why. Right from your toes to the ends of your hair, [everything] stand [sic]. You are in complete shock. Your heart palpitates, you don't understand and you are aware of people looking at you... you can compare it to hell,' described the actor on *Tere Mere Beach Mein*, a talk show hosted by Farah Khan.

Early on in his life, Roshan knew he wanted to be an actor and despite his impediment, set about doing everything he could to accomplish that dream. Over the years, he worked consistently on his speech therapy, besides watching the proceedings on film sets. He also made it a point to learn from the superstars, Anil Kapoor, Salman Khan and Shah Rukh Khan among others, who acted in his father Rakesh Roshan's films. In preparation, he worked as an unaccredited assistant on his father's films for the longest time, even sweeping floors and fetching coffee on occasions.

As per one of his tweets, 'Nothing is derogatory if you don't allow it to derogate you. If you choose to stop feeling insulted, it ceases to feel like an insult. Think about it.' Roshan's way of overcoming a hindrance is to work really hard at it. As he did with his speech defect till it disappeared. He may be a widely acknowledged superstar now, but still works hard, reading his dialogues aloud to get the perfect shot.

Kangana Ranaut, his co-star in *Kites* and *Krrish 3*, once mentioned how conscientious he was during the filming of *Krrish 3* to ensure that the scene was just right. Instead of being afraid of being laughed at, he concentrates on his efforts to improve. Overcoming one's weaknesses, he has always maintained, gives great strength. He should know! It has earned him the respect of his colleagues both within and outside the industry. His own explanation of it is fairly simple, 'Maybe I have so many faults that people who watch me spend time rectifying them think I am perfecting my shots. I have deep passion for my work and a lot of broken tools that I employ. I need to spend more time for each film which is why I can't do ten films a year.'

Everybody has limitations, but where most people allow themselves to remain that way, Roshan did not. It is this ability to win over difficulties against all odds that separates an achiever from the crowd.

LOOK STUPID, LOOK FOOLISH

'Really rejoice in being yourself. Have your own drumbeat.'
—KIM CATTRALL

Ask Roshan about his ability to dance like a dervish and he says, 'Don't worry about people watching. It's fine even if you are not moving to the rules some people have made. Make your own rules. Look stupid, look foolish.' It's a personal philosophy that he has successfully used over the years to help tide him over self-consciousness.

Everybody fears being laughed at, but when acting is one's career, being made fun of or scorned has to be taken in one's stride. Roshan, despite being a skinny teenager with a speech defect, learnt to deal with it. While the ordeal of being laughed at in school was traumatic, it did not stop him from planning a life in the movies.

In an article carried in *The Indian Express*, he mentioned that he used to be petrified of viva voce tests as the other students would laugh at him. So he would bunk school, pretending to be ill, or feign some other excuse and stay away. Over a period of time, he slowly built up confidence.

He had a very clear picture of his shortcomings, but that did not make him shrug off his dreams. Instead, it motivated him to blaze his own trail, starting with *Kaho Naa... Pyaar Hai*. The film established him as a superstar who could act well, dance like a dream and look divine—the complete showbiz package! In his early films he chose to conceal the extra thumb on his hand, but with time he has become comfortable displaying a physical feature that may not be entirely flattering. After a photoshoot for a fashion magazine, he tweeted, tongue firmly in cheek, 'Thanks guys for your feedback on Harpers! Katrina is fabulous, missed my thumb though. Art team must have thought it ugly. Forgive and forget.'

> Life is not about holding the best cards but about how you play the cards you have been dealt with. Everything of your body—your mind, emotions, speech, ability to observe; are all tools.

An ability to let things rest lightly on your shoulders only strengthens you as a person. Roshan's ability to let ridicule slide off his back has helped him make the transition from the proverbial caterpillar to butterfly.

BE AN EXPLORER

'All those hours of exploring have made me more resilient and confident.'—DAVID SUZUKI

Unwilling to rest after the runaway success of his debut film, Roshan boldly went ahead with projects that he had signed before he turned superstar, regardless of the fact that he ran the risk of failure. Be it a film like *Mission Kashmir* (2000) where he played a young Kashmiri driven to terrorism; or later, *Koi... Mil Gaya* (2003), in which he was a physically and mentally challenged boy; a historical, *Jodhaa Akbar* (2008) where he essayed the role of Mughal Emperor Akbar; or *Guzaarish* (2010), where he played a paraplegic, Roshan is always up for a challenge. But the most daring of all these adventures was *Kites*, a multilingual (English/Hindi/Spanish) film from Bollywood, that aimed at creating a space for Hindi films in the international market. In fact, Roshan roped in Hollywood producer–director Brett Ratner to edit the film for the Western audience. Exploration of the unknown, according to him, is essential for growth.

My personal quest is to find out what I am about. How far can I push myself? What is my true extreme potential? I want to evolve and grow and the only way to do that is by challenging yourself, putting yourself through those fires from which you come out a stronger man. I want my story to be the greatest. Chapters of strife and struggle in my life, even self-inflicted, will make me achieve what I am striving for.

'I am an adventurer by nature. I am an explorer in my heart and to be a true explorer you need the courage and will of iron because it's easy to find something you might get addicted to. But you have to have the will to let go and swing to the other end of the spectrum to explore something else. That's why my films range from *Dhoom* to *Krissh* to *Guzaarish* and *Fiza*. That is what keeps me going. Keeps me driven, keeps me enthusiastic about what I am doing. Also I feel it's so easy to keep doing things that you know work—*Dhoom*, *Krissh*—it's easy to keep doing that but where are you truly going? I want to leave behind an example for the next generation of actors that don't be afraid to experiment. See how much I have gained from it. If you are determined enough, you will come out clean and happy,' he held forth in an interview with *Screen*.

To step into unknown territory is easier said than done. Many choose the easy way out and live life in the slow lane. But greatness comes only to those who forge ahead on paths where others fear to tread. Roshan continues to look for those uncharted realms with every step; he knows in his heart that an impediment exists only to be overcome.

USE REJECTION TO MAKE YOU FLY

'A rejection is nothing more than a necessary step in the pursuit of success.'—BO BENNETT

There was a phase in Roshan's career, soon after his unprecedented debut, when his films were falling like nine pins. Vidhu Vinod Chopra's *Mission Kashmir* provided some respite but others such as *Fiza* (2000), *Yaadein* (2001), *Mujhse Dosti Karoge!* (2002), *Aap Mujhe Achche Lagne Lage* (2002) and *Main*

Prem Ki Deewani Hoon (2003), met with lukewarm responses. It prompted a film magazine to put him on the cover with a headline that said 'Finished'.

The death knell of his career had been sounded. Roshan, however, did not let it deter him. Instead, he processed his feelings about the rejection and used it to fuel his efforts. When asked about it, he had a simple explanation: he had not believed the magazines when they called him a phenomenon, so he would treat their rejection in the same fashion and continue to perfect his craft. The magazine cover announcing the end of his career only served to further fuel his ambition.

'Fear gives you wings. For me it's like fluttering around in my room to find a starting point. And once that happens, I don't fear anything at all,' avers Roshan.

To be dropped suddenly from a great height into an abyss is not enviable. Roshan's life has been about struggling with obstacles, so he has learnt to treat each fall as a foothold to climb higher. Such diligence and audacity is truly commendable and worthy of emulation.

TRY AND TRY AGAIN

'Behind every successful man is a trail made of determination, a path of overcoming failures, several rest areas of prayer time and friendly mentors pointing out the direction.'—DOUG SEATON

Roshan's approach to the challenges in his life is rather philosophical. Rather than crying over spilt milk, he believes in making the best of what he has. It explains his laborious efforts at everything he does. So even if a scene just has him walking, he will never be content with one take, says his father, director–producer Rakesh Roshan. He keeps at it till he is completely satisfied.

As a teenager, Roshan had a skinny physique, a far cry from the body required of an aspiring film star. In those days the prevalent look of a Hindi film hero was the buff version popularized by Sanjay Dutt and Salman Khan. The story goes that Roshan took pointers from Khan (the superstar was acting in one of Rakesh Roshan's films at that time) and slogged endlessly till he achieved his dream body. And the results were there for all to see!

'Life is not about holding the best cards but about how you play the cards you have been dealt with. Everything of your body [sic]—your mind, emotions, speech, ability to observe; are all tools,' he says.

Physical transformation starts in the mind. As soon as Roshan decided that he had to change his physique, he set about it with the faith that it could be achieved. His perfect body is a reflection of his determined mind. Our resolutions never take off because of the wavering in our heads. In order to persevere despite heavy odds, one has to win the battles against one's own weaknesses first, something that Roshan has done time and again.

PUSH THE LIMITS

'The only limits are, as always, those of vision.'
—*JAMES BROUGHTON*

Hrithik Roshan's body is cited as the ultimate body beautiful in the film industry and beyond, with everyone vying for a chiselled physique like his. However, he almost came within an inch of losing it when he was beset with back (slipped disc) and knee injuries. To make matters worse, he was advised bed rest and consequently gained weight. Yet another injury sustained during the shooting of *Agneepath* added to the list of challenges when Roshan was preparing for *Krrish 3*. He had to engage a fitness trainer, who drove him relentlessly to get back into shape and on his feet.

'My personal quest is to find out what I am about. How far can I push myself? What is my true extreme potential? I want to evolve and grow and the only way to do that is by challenging yourself, putting yourself through those fires from which you come out a stronger man. I want my story to be the greatest. Chapters of strife and struggle in my life, even self-inflicted, will make me achieve what I am striving for.'

> Resting on past laurels and being deluded is not me. I feel proud, privileged and scared because who wants to lose being where you are?

The steely resolve that one requires to overcome a physical or any other setback is a prerequisite for achieving success. Roshan's highs and lows have one common feature that has propelled his growth—his ability to relentlessly push himself beyond the limit.

REALITY CHECK

'We must accept finite disappointment, but never lose infinite hope.'—MARTIN LUTHER KING, JR

At the outset of his career, Roshan received a euphoric welcome that surprised him. He would insist that he was not deserving of the hysteria around him. When Simi Garewal questioned him about it (on her television show *Rendezvous with Simi Garewal*) he summed it up rather succinctly, 'I worked for fifty rupees and got a hundred rupees in return.' He always maintained that he was prepared to return the extra bit that had come his way. Later in his career, when the scales tilted against him, he accepted the hardships gracefully as the universe's way of balancing, while remaining grateful for all good things in his life.

'I could not have asked for a better run—it started off with *Kaho Naa... Pyaar Hai* and I start my second decade with *Guzaarish*. I can't be more thankful. I have seen some great successes and some failures both of which have added to my life. In the successes I saw people dance, throw coins, scream, shout, clap but I never felt what I felt after *Guzaarish*. It has got me so much love from the industry, my seniors, contemporaries... I mean it's so overwhelming that I need to keep a check on myself. I need to take just as much as I need to motivate myself for the next one. The rest I need to pass on. This kind of appreciation can murder the artistic sanity of the person, but yes I think it's a great balance between box office and great appreciation, which I have received. If I would have got everything, I probably would have gone mad.'

Only a person standing in a valley truly appreciates the height of the mountain before him. Understanding this phenomenon enables one to attempt an uphill task, relishing the challenge rather than groaning under its weight.

HRITHIK ROSHAN'S MANUAL TO A BEAUTIFUL LIFE

Hrithik Roshan has a backstory that could inspire anyone who considers himself or herself average and mediocre. It's almost like a fairy tale detailing all the hardships that the prince goes through before he defeats the ogre. Only, the ogres in this story are the limitations within himself. Be it his childhood stammering problem, a slipped disc or a spate of flops, he has surmounted them all; slaying demons, both within and without, with distinction. Here's why the hero's struggles have all added up to a splendid triumph:

☆ **Acknowledgement slip:** Several times the bigger problem lies in pretending that a handicap or an obstacle does not exist. Fortunately for Roshan, his stammering problem was not left unattended. From a young age he displayed the resilience to face his handicap, persevering with his therapy so that he would not be laughed at. Even now during interviews, if he happens to trip on a word, instead of withdrawing into an embarrassed silence, Roshan repeats it slowly and patiently till he gets it right.

☆ **Blessing in disguise:** Sometimes, what appears a curse can turn out to be a blessing. In overcoming his speech problem, Roshan addressed quite a few major aspects of acting itself—he knew early on that he wanted to pursue an acting career and in overcoming the fear of looking or sounding clumsy and working on his diction, he began to perfect the craft way before he began his formal training as an actor. It helps, therefore, to not think of a disadvantage as insurmountable, but as an opportunity to improve.

☆ **Courage:** To put oneself out there despite shortcomings is tough. One has to marshal courage to go through the ordeal. Roshan displayed great fortitude in his early years by facing his fears. Now it has given him wings—he is not scared of making unconventional choices in his work, a huge advantage in the creative field. His ability to experiment with risky, out-of-the-box ideas have earned him great appreciation.

☆ **Preparedness:** Accustomed to hardships from early years, perhaps due to his father Rakesh Roshan's fluctuating fortunes in the movie business—they had to live in a shared apartment, and on occasions even sleep on the floor—Roshan has never shied away from hard work. As he said once on Twitter, 'Don't sleep hoping everything will go well tomorrow. Sleep with full prep to attack new problems tomorrow. Stay ready. Know they'll come and you'll conquer them one by one.'

KARAN JOHAR
Diplomacy and Tact

'I always prefer to believe the best of everybody.
It saves so much trouble.'

—RUDYARD KIPLING

If there were an Indian version of the book *How to Win Friends and Influence People*, it would probably be authored by Karan Johar, the film industry's go-to guy for all seasons. Be it the Bachchans or the Khan triumvirate, the Gen X or the Gen Next, Johar is the common factor that binds them professionally and personally. From being the life of the party at friends' sangeet ceremonies to hosting professional arch-rivals on his television chat show *Koffee With Karan* (2004–), from interviewing Oscar-winning director Ang Lee to accepting an olive branch from fellow film-maker Ram Gopal Varma, he has done it all with the aplomb and ease of a seasoned diplomat.

Dharma Productions, started by his father Yash Johar, is going from strength to strength under Johar's leadership. With a plethora of films starring India's biggest stars and industry veterans, while also giving new-age directors and actors a chance, it is a testimony to all that he brings to the table. His fortieth birthday party was a high-wattage gathering of Bollywood's top brass, reflecting the growth of his company from a standalone production unit to a boutique creative house with 'the ambitions of a studio'.

While replicating Johar's charm might be difficult, a few hard-nosed, practical principles he follows can certainly help a socially challenged person.

BE A PEOPLE'S PERSON

'Creative collaboration is awesome.'—ALICIA SILVERSTONE

The affable film-maker has always admitted to being a people's person. 'I like to like people, it's easier,' he says. Liking people or enjoying other people's company is a good starting point. It certainly helps when you are in the film business, a highly collaborative profession. The inner coterie of Johar's professional world comprises old friends—Apurva Mehta, CEO, Dharma Productions, is a school friend—and most of the directors Dharma has launched—Punit Malhotra, Tarun Mansukhani, Ayan Mukerji, Shakun Batra, Sonam Nair, Karan Malhotra—have a work history with the company. They have all assisted on Dharma films.

> Actors are the most insecure bunch of people in the world. No matter how many movies they do, they are still looking for that nod of approval. They need hand-holding.

However, that does not stop Johar from opening the doors to those who haven't. Over the last few years, in the creative interest of the company, he has moved away from his earlier practice of collaborating only with those who have worked for Dharma. Directors Rensil D'Silva and Rohit Shetty are examples of outsiders who have joined the Dharma fold. Johar's inclusiveness does the trick, expanding the creative and commercial repertoire of his company.

In putting together a disparate group of people who work as individuals with a common goal, he stands out as an example of a canny, people-oriented motivator who leverages differing personalities for the best possible output.

DIFFERENT STROKES FOR DIFFERENT FOLKS

'Coming together is a beginning; keeping together is progress; working together is success.'—HENRY FORD

Johar has a great understanding of the different expectations and requirements that people may have. He decodes them instinctively and interacts accordingly. With film stars, the rules are different from those that apply to directors. Of his ability to manage the former, he says, 'Actors are the most insecure bunch of people in the world. No matter how many movies they do, they are still looking for that nod of approval. They need hand-holding.'

In fact, Dharma's reputation for treating its stars well dates back to Johar's father Yash Johar, who shared a wonderful rapport with all the leading actors of his time—Amitabh Bachchan, Sadhana, Sridevi and Sanjay Dutt, to name a few. And Johar has taken that legacy forward. Leading actor Kareena Kapoor vouches for his unique way of handling stars. 'It's a pleasure to work with Karan because, like Yash uncle, he really knows how to treat his stars.'

> What's happening around me, who likes or dislikes each other, is not important anymore. I am fulfilling my commitments as a human being and as a professional. I will always say and do the right things and be protocol-friendly in my dealings.

Directors, on the other hand, Johar believes, should be allowed to take the lead and fly with their ideas. He is extremely supportive of Dharma's young brigade with resources. 'I cast according to a director's demands. If a director does not want somebody, I go with his choice because I feel a director should not be lumbered with anyone—a technician or star—that he's not happy with. I always tell my directors to aim for the sky. What's the harm in trying?'

Anyone who has met Johar will tell you that he is courteous

and charming; he displays an innate sensitivity to the person across the table, a boon in the film business where egos are fragile and the famous artistic temperament a constant. Newbie Alia Bhatt whom he launched in his directorial venture *Student of the Year* (2013) said of him, 'I was so full of insecurities during the project but Karan didn't let me feel that I was terrible. When I was not getting a scene right, he would make sure that I understood it but not in a way that said, "You are so stupid, you can't get it."'

Johar explains, 'I am a keen observer so I understand the personal issues in their heads. I enjoy it. I like people. I don't have family except for mom and me so I don't have to worry about spending time with [my] family. I can sit here and work. I get involved in every department. I am not inaccessible.'

DON'T CARRY OTHER PEOPLE'S EQUATIONS INTO YOUR OWN

'Diplomacy: the art of restraining power!'—HENRY KISSINGER

One of the questions Johar often faces is about his ability to be friends with different groups of people, not all them amicably disposed towards each other. He shares a great equation with Aamir, Salman and Shah Rukh Khan without ruffling any feathers. 'What's happening around me, who likes or dislikes each other, is not important anymore. I am fulfilling my commitments as a human being and as a professional. I will always say and do the right things and be protocol-friendly in my dealings.'

It is a difficult proposition not to take sides in an industry dominated by supersized egos, but by taking a neutral stand, Johar sends a clear message that he is open and accepting of everyone. People in the industry have also accepted Johar's principle of non-alignment, of being his own person, who adheres to his own equations with people.

APPRECIATE THE GOOD IN OTHERS

'Never hate your enemies. It affects your judgement.'
—MARIO PUZO

In an industry where acknowledging someone else's creative genius is generally unheard of, Johar stands out for his generous praise of peers and colleagues, even if they don't count among his favourite people. Despite his run-ins with Ram Gopal Varma and their constant jibes at each other, he has always maintained that Varma is a fine director who has given Hindi cinema some of its finest films. He has also doffed his hat to fellow directors Rajkumar Hirani, Zoya Akhtar and Sooraj Barjatya, none of them affiliated with his production company, as the finest directing talents in the country.

Such seemingly simple gestures hide great merit. For starters, it generates tremendous goodwill in his professional circles, which in a business as collaborative as the movies is a huge plus. Especially when he is a television host, producer and director all rolled into one. Johar is that rare television host who has had former and current divas, Madhuri Dixit and Sonakshi Sinha; competing colleagues, Lara Dutta and Katrina Kaif; as well as a couple, Aishwarya and Abhishek Bachchan, come together on his television show to share their secrets!

The ability to focus on the good in people empowers and cloaks one with the confidence and positivity needed to deal with them socially, regardless of one's personal equations.

DON'T JUDGE PEOPLE BY THEIR SUCCESS OR FAILURE

'Success is not final; failure is not fatal. It is the courage to continue that counts.'—WINSTON CHURCHILL

'A Friday can change your life' goes an old film industry saying. And as any film star or director will tell you, it's true! In addition to your bank balance and future prospects, success plays a hand in determining your friends too.

Johar, a stickler for principles, remains a steady support. Actress Kajol, known to be his friend since childhood, continues to be a part of his films even if it is for a guest appearance, regardless of the fate of the other films she stars in. It's none too different in the professional realm either. Rensil D'Silva, who directed *Kurbaan* (2009), was not shown the door when the film failed to work. Instead, he has stayed on for another project under Johar's banner.

While this may seem foolhardy to many, it is a positive step towards building loyal work relationships that last over years in different capacities, regardless of the success or failure of an individual. It adds immeasurable goodwill.

'Failure is never something that motivates or demotivates me. It does not reflect someone's talent,' reiterates Johar.

Last heard, Johar's Dharma Productions, with one or two exceptions, has

> How can one keep silent when we are affected as an industry? I feel very strongly about it. If I keep quiet then what is the point of having achieved a certain position? If you are not leveraging the authority that you have garnered, what are you doing anyway?

an almost 100 per cent retention rate among its creative staff!

Johar's belief is that people—even the bright and smart ones—fail sometimes, but given a chance and support, they can succeed again. This earns him tremendous loyalty and goodwill, a must-have for any team leader.

SPEAK UP

'He who does not have the courage to speak up for his own rights, cannot earn the respect of others.'—RENE C. TORRES

Though he is seen as diplomatic, Johar steps out of his comfort zone and takes up for others should the need arise, as he did for actor–director Kamal Haasan when his film *Vishwaroopam* (2013) was banned by the state government in Tamil Nadu. Having faced a similar situation with *My Name Is Khan*, Johar understands the vulnerability of an actor–producer on the day before a film's release. The nightmare of the experience and the subsequent losses in collection have steered the course of his present actions.

'How can one keep silent when we are affected as an industry? I feel very strongly about it. If I keep quiet then what is the point of having achieved a certain position? If you are not leveraging the authority that you have garnered, what are you doing anyway? We all have responsibilities to our family, our community, and our surroundings. Sometimes I can't do anything single-handedly but if my words can resonate with even a small percentage of people then I would have achieved an optimum of my position today.'

Johar believes that within the workspace it is important to stand up and extend a helping hand to colleagues in their time of need. Speaking in one voice not only supports the individual facing the crisis but also strengthens the entire community. It encourages all members to step forward and assist those in a vulnerable position. As an eminent member of the fraternity who takes the lead in supporting colleagues, Johar is widely respected both within and outside the film industry.

BE INVOLVED

'You must get involved to have an impact.'—NAPOLEON HILL

'I am generally a people's person and I am always there for people in my life. For me, my life, my company and work are integral,' is Johar's summary of his people-friendly ways.

Despite a very hectic schedule with a series of film shoots on the floor, collaborations and co-productions, Johar makes it a point to attend all personal events, as well as a significant number of business forums. He remains involved with a whole spectrum of fraternity members. From choreographer Bosco's celebration party to Big B's seventieth birthday bash, Johar is an integral part of it all, remaining his affable and charming self. In fact, he was the Master of Ceremonies for Amitabh Bachchan's birthday bash and his dance was reportedly the highlight of Aishwarya Rai and Abhishek Bachchan's sangeet!

As a co-chair of FICCI Frames, he has been responsible for pulling in newer stars like Sonakshi Sinha, Ranbir Kapoor and Vidya Balan among others for the platform that aims to promote business growth within the film industry. Johar also supports young acting talent—Alia Bhatt, Sidharth Malhotra and Varun Dhawan—not just launching them but also guiding them in their choice of films, looking into their future projects and so on.

Johar's personal involvement in fraternity matters has added tremendously to his professional profile, as also his knowledge of the sector. From someone who used to sign his cheques with a 'Love, Karan' to talking about business verticals, putting out multiple softwares and engineering several co-productions, he has certainly come a long way.

> With people I know, I am straightforward. My diplomacy is for people I have to be diplomatic with. If I don't care about somebody I would be diplomatic. Why should I upset somebody who is not working with me?

In seeking opportunities to collaborate with different film-makers such as Anurag Kashyap, Dibakar Banerjee and Zoya Akhtar for the cause of cinema (as he did with *Bombay Talkies* [2013]) Johar allows himself exposure to different working styles and creative influences. It also connects him to a wide spectrum of people.

Johar has a clear understanding that as one grows in one's profession, one also becomes responsible to the professional community at large. The idea of giving back to one's profession is important for every human being's development, as well as for society.

FORGIVE AND FORGET

*'The weak can never forgive.
Forgiveness is the attribute of the strong.'*
—MAHATMA GANDHI

'My father once said to me, "If you have upset someone, say

sorry. There is no harm in saying so",' mentioned Johar in an interview when I quizzed him about giving in when objections were raised about the word 'Bombay' being used instead of 'Mumbai' in his home production *Wake Up Sid*.

It's a lesson that he assiduously follows. When Ram Gopal Varma poked fun at him on social networking sites, taking a dig at Johar's films, Johar replied in the same vein, calling Varma's horror films like *Phoonk* (2008) unwatchable. Their exchange of acerbic comments continued for a while. Yet, when Varma decided to call a truce by extending an invitation to Johar for the screening of *The Attacks of 26/11*(2013), Johar was gracious enough to accept his invitation and clear the air.

Speaking of the incident he said, 'Both of us have an inherent sense of humour and those remarks were not out of some hatred or animosity we have for each other. It's just some fun we were having. I don't think he likes any of my movies but there are many of his that I have liked—*Satya* [1998], *Company* [2002] and *Sarkar* [2005]. In fact there is a whole zone of films that I think he pioneered. For me to love someone's work, it is not necessary that they love mine.'

Yet another instance of his ability to move on was when he made up with actress Priyanka Chopra after a verbal duel. In 2012, when an article stating that Chopra was being ignored by star wives and a certain director (hinting at Johar) appeared, the usually unflappable Johar saw red. He retaliated with an angry outburst on Twitter, saying that goodness should not be messed around with.

However, a few days later, in a display of both maturity and magnanimity, Johar personally invited the actress for his fortieth birthday celebration party. When explaining the turn of events and change of heart, he was rather candid.

'There was an article that came out wherein I felt wronged. But, I should have picked up the phone and spoken to her [Priyanka] instead of going to print [sic] because I ended [up] doing the same thing she had done. I felt very stupid, so four days before I celebrated my fortieth birthday, I picked up the phone and called her and said, "Listen, I am very sorry. I overreacted. So please come, you have been a part of the production house and we have had a perfect working relationship." I realized it was a mistake and I won't repeat it because it was completely out of character. I was angrier with my own self, because I've not been raised by my parents to behave like this. My mom was very upset and told me, "This is not who you are,"' explained Johar.

The ability to forgive, if not forget, is perhaps the one trait that sets a man apart. For Johar, this is a cherished value.

DISCERNING DIPLOMACY

'In the world of diplomacy, some things are better left unsaid.'
—LINCOLN CHAFEE

Among the things that Kareena Kapoor credits best buddy Johar with is being forthright. According to her, it's the reason they get along.

Surrounded by scores of people that he interacts with in varying capacities—actors, journalists, studio heads, television channel heads besides fans and hordes of aspiring actors/directors/technicians who desire to be on his team, Johar's alternate display of diplomacy and frankness makes tremendous sense. His stance is simple enough.

'With people I know, I am straightforward. My diplomacy

is for people I have to be diplomatic with. If I don't care about somebody I would be diplomatic. Why should I upset somebody who is not working with me? If I care for somebody, say someone I work with, and I don't like the first cut, I would say it sucks. I will be as honest as that. I will be straightforward and professional with people I work with.'

The person who speaks words that bear no malice will always be liked, but the person who is discerning with truth is revered. Picking an opportune time and candidate for frank-speak is a feat very few can pull off; Johar's practice of it is impeccable!

STATESMANSHIP, THE KARAN JOHAR WAY

Johar's ability to be tactful and diplomatic is perhaps almost as well-known as his glamorous films. His people skills and deft handling of tricky situations is a talent he has acquired from his father Yash Johar. Only that Johar has honed it to perfection! Given his innate ability to retain old associates and bring in new names into the Dharma fold, it is no wonder that he has creative alliances with the best in the business.

☆ **Personal touch:** The movie business, though it has moved towards a studio system, still functions primarily on the basis of relationships and rapport. Johar's easy-going charm and ability to get along with a wide spectrum of people is a sure-fire advantage. His composed approach and tact go a long way in convincing people to work with him—a fact substantiated by the impressive list of people signing up for professional ventures with him.

☆ **Selective company:** A series of fortuitous developments, such as his television show *Koffee With Karan* and his presence on the committees for powerful industry forums such as FICCI Frames, have lent an aspirational value to both Johar's company and personal association with him. Of course, this coupled with the inherent flair for appreciating virtues in even those on the other side of the fence has worked wonders for Johar and his company. Smartly alternating between being choosy and yet open to talent across spectra works like a charm for those he shares a professional equation with.

- ☆ **Tough love**: Let's face it, when you are working in a creative field with the biggest names in business, fragile egos come with the territory. However, to be effective, one has to be the iron hand in the velvet glove; something that Johar has pulled off enviably on most occasions. While generous and giving with resources and financial support as well as bringing the best actors and technicians on board, Johar is firm with his decisions. Long ago when Kareena Kapoor, one of his best friends, demanded an acting fee that was beyond the budget for *Kal Ho Naa Ho* (2003), Johar passed her up for another actress. Of course they have patched up since and Kapoor is back in the Dharma fold.
- ☆ **Sound judgment**: Success and failure are such an intrinsic part of the Bollywood roulette that resting one's equations purely on commercial worth is fraught with danger. Talent and emotional equity is the yardstick for Johar, who maintains associations beyond the hit and flop drill.

SALMAN KHAN

Generosity

'You have not lived today until you have done something for someone who can never repay you.'

—John Bunyan

Mention Salman Khan's name and two things come to mind—*Dabangg*'s Chulbul Pandey and the Being Human charity initiatives. A far cry from his earlier bratty avatar, when he made headlines for all the wrong reasons.

Although right from the get-go Khan has been famous for his volatile lifestyle, matters hit an all-time low in 2002, with reports of an alleged case of drunk driving. A few men sleeping on the pavement outside Mumbai's American Express Bakery were accidentally run over by the actor's car. In fact, a slideshow of the headlines from 2002 to 2005 would have convinced even the most ardent of fans that Salman Khan was Bollywood's ultimate wild child.

Fast-forward to the years between 2008 and 2013, and the story of the brash Khan had completely changed. All with good reason, of course. For starters, he rose to the top of his game with an impressive list of hit films—*Wanted* (2009), *Dabangg* (2010), *Dabangg 2* (2012), *Ready* (2011), *Bodyguard* (2011) and *Ek Tha Tiger* (2012). The film industry was compelled to acknowledge that Salman was definitely numero uno at the box office stakes. He was also unanimously anointed the presiding deity of the Bollywood 100-crore club.

If that was not enough, he cemented his position with a canny deal of ₹500 crore with the Star (India Pvt. Ltd) television network for the satellite rights of all his films released over a five-year period. At the last count, he continues to be the most wanted brand ambassador for products ranging from colas to candies.

Another prominent aspect about the new, improved Salman Khan is the Being Human Foundation, the NGO established by him for poor people who need medical assistance.

The Being Human Foundation, according to a *Business Today* report, is already a 100-crore brand, ever-expanding its scope of charitable activities. Besides supporting the cause of healthcare and education, the NGO even sent 2,500 tankers of water to drought-affected farmers in Maharashtra in 2013. These initiatives, according to those who know Khan well, are not an affectation. Rather, they are an extension of his personality.

Khan's father, noted scriptwriter Salim Khan, reiterates that his superstar son is a good-natured person, who may have lacked the maturity earlier to handle personal relationships, a shortcoming that led him to be demonized by the media. And although Khan chooses to differ, the fact is that over the years, he has transformed into a calmer person with a handle on his celebrity status and the situations that arise from it. In stark contrast to his past diffidence, he treats queries about his personal life with humour and a lightness that was missing earlier.

Success makes for heady copy but in Khan's case, it is his remarkable journey from the time that he could perceivably

---

I guess it [his charity] would have to be [due to] lessons I have learnt as a child. I think moral science classes in school taught me all of it. Things like 'help the needy, try to be as correct as possible, bend backwards for other people, arrogance is not good, badtameezi nahin karna, thank you bolna, sorry bolna, respect dena, don't take bullshit, don't give bullshit'. These are the only lessons I have learnt and I have lived my life by them. *Uske baad jo grey areas hain woh dheere dheere karke seekhte gaye but jo major areas hain, woh yehi hai.*

do no right to now when he can do no wrong, that has caught everyone's imagination.

So how did Khan bring about this phenomenal change?

CHARITY BEGINS AT HOME

'Every good act is charity. A man's true wealth hereafter is the good that he does in this world to his fellows.'—MOLIERE

The memory of my first meeting with superstar Salman Khan at Mumbai's Mehboob Studio is rather vivid—there was a huge crowd outside Salman Bhai's (as he is fondly referred to by his zillion fans) vanity van waiting to catch a glimpse of him. A visually impaired boy in his teens stood patiently, waiting for his turn to meet the star. He was lucky; once done with the shot, Khan obliged the boy with his autograph and posed for a photo. He even gave the boy a patient hearing while the child sang for his favourite actor!

Salim Khan says that even as a young boy, Salman Khan always displayed sensitivity towards the underprivileged, lending those in need a helping hand. Whether it was helping a boy from the neighbouring fishing village buy a fishnet or

---

> It is not enough to just have a big star. You have to give him things to do that suit his personality. Sometimes you go wrong because your own ego, ghamand or pride takes over but then later you realize that also. You think that I will be able to pull it off but then you realize ki yeh zyaada ho raha hai, isko kam karo. But yes, sometimes you do get carried away.

---

taking accident victims to the hospital, Khan was always at the forefront.

When the principal of Stanislaus High School (Khan's alma mater) urged students to get lunch for the underprivileged students who could not bring tiffin boxes to school, Khan checked with his mother if he could help and the very next day brought all ten boys home for lunch! Given his generous nature, it is no surprise that Galaxy Apartments at Bandra Bandstand, where he resides with his parents, is inundated with requests from the needy. It started with him giving money to poor people requiring medical aid and is now a massively organized effort under the Being Human umbrella aimed to help people for various causes. Several people undertake charitable activities, but two features set Khan's efforts apart.

The first is that his endeavours are an extension of his regular life. For instance, when he organized a special screening of his film *Ready* for underprivileged children, he went to each theatre (where the shows were being held) to meet and interact with them. Over the years, Khan has been very supportive of the Cancer Patients Aid Association, meeting with terminally ill patients, especially kids. He even volunteered to become a bone marrow donor (usually difficult to procure), in order to help cancer-afflicted children. The second is his success in making Being Human sustainable and self-reliant.

Ask him about his charity fetish and he says, 'I don't know why people make such a big deal of it. I guess it [the charity] would have to be [due to] lessons I have learnt as a child. I think moral science classes in school taught me all of it. Things like "help the needy, try to be as correct as possible, bend backwards for other people, arrogance is not good, badtameezi nahin karna, thank you bolna, sorry bolna, respect dena, don't take bullshit, don't give bullshit". These are the only lessons I have learnt and I have lived my life by them. *Uske baad jo grey areas hain woh dheere dheere karke seekhte gaye but jo major areas hain, woh yehi hai.'*

The positivity that one feels after performing an act of kindness melts all angst. In Khan's case, a deep sense of caring for the underprivileged remains the cornerstone of his upbringing. In turn he receives the love and blessings of many. Khan's innate goodness has carried him through many a crisis and kept him firmly perched in his audience's good books.

WORKING ON STARDOM

'Continuous effort—not strength or intelligence—is the key to unlocking our potential.'—WINSTON CHURCHILL

Let's face it, when Khan walks into a room, he owns the space. His swagger, the motley group accompanying him (his manager, personal bodyguard and occasionally his dogs), forewarn you of his arrival. On screen, it is no different. Of late, the audience has started warming up to the star's presence even before he utters a line. Be that as it may, Khan, after a spate of earlier films that flopped despite his star presence, has understood the importance of signing the right projects that utilize as well as enhance his stardom. Unlike in the past when he agreed to almost any film proposed by friends, Khan now assesses its potential for him as an actor before giving his consent. It may or may not be someone he's known for a long time. Kabir Khan, the director of *Ek Tha Tiger*, was not an old pal, but Khan liked him and more significantly liked the script of the film enough to give it his nod of approval.

'It is not enough to just have a big star. You have to give him things to do that suit his personality. Sometimes you go wrong because your own ego, ghamand or pride takes over but then later you realize that also. You think that I will be able to pull it off but then you realize ki yeh zyaada ho raha hai, isko kam karo. But, yes sometimes you do get carried away,' reasons Khan.

His father attributes this phase of his superstardom to both experience and improvement in his choice of films. According to Salim Khan, his eldest-born often chose films for the wrong reasons—to help friends or producers who claimed that they did not have enough money to put a film together. More often than not, such ventures failed to benefit anyone because they were neither planned nor executed properly. Having learnt from past experience, Khan now sets aside his generosity for the Being Human Foundation that has seen unprecedented response from individuals and corporate houses alike. As for his movies, he bases his decisions on pertinent factors, such as the merit of the script, the director's calibre and so on. A successful film that is appreciated by the audience strengthens his star value besides ensuring good returns for the producer and director of the film, making it a win-win situation for all concerned.

According to friend and colleague Anil Kapoor, Khan has started working harder on his acting and dancing skills too, infusing his trademark style with such energy and zest that it becomes inimitable. 'Now, I am not going to touch anything which I am not excited about. Even if it is unnees-bees. Let someone else take it up and turn it into the biggest hit. It should always be a film that I want to go into theatres and watch,' Khan says.

The flipside of generosity is that people can take advantage of one's goodness. A smart way to practise generosity is to compartmentalize it and be discerning. In Khan's case, this new approach has helped his charity as well as his acting career, making it a win-win situation.

BUSINESS 'WISE'

'If you don't drive your business, you will be driven out of business.'—B.C. FORBES

Known to be something of a bleeding heart, Khan frequently waived his remuneration when producers cited shortage of funds. It turned out to be a convenient excuse for some wily persons, a fact he finally wisened up to. Soon after, Salim Khan began to look after his son's finances to ensure that he was not being taken for a ride. However, for business negotiations pertaining to his varying portfolios—films, television, brand endorsements, events and more, Khan signed up with a market-savvy business manager.

Khan's new business savvy was on display in turning the Celebrity Cricket League matches, managed by brother Sohail Khan, into a success. He has kept away from the IPL and created a strong brand equity for Celebrity Cricket League, by leveraging his star power and goodwill with friends and fellow actors, making the matches exciting and watchable affairs.

Then there is the famous ₹500 crore deal with Star (India Pvt. Ltd) for the rights of the films he makes over the next five years, a first for a film star. Considering his popularity among the television-viewing audience—his films are among the highest rated on television—Khan was canny in inking the deal. Not only does it give him a huge corpus of funds for film-making, it maximizes his star value by expanding his audience base.

One of the conditions he puts forward when endorsing products is that the company should make a contribution to his charity as well. Khan,

> It's one life yaar, whatever is there in my destiny will happen. You go through situations and come out, sometimes you get stuck. Life is one big story and you should have a superb story to tell.

with the help of his team, has come up with numerous innovative business methods. Being Human's revenue model, for instance, is based on royalties from the sale of Being Human merchandise, not donations.

Khan also picked up a small stake in the travel portal Yatra.com, ensuring that one rupee from every transaction would go to the foundation.

'One rupee, I believe, is very big number. *Sau mein se ek rupiya chala gaya toh it does not make a difference par jab hazaron, karoron mein aata hai to hazaaro karor ho jata hai.* That's what we are doing—we take one rupee per transaction [for Yatra.com]. We can do 30-40 transactions per day. It works up to a big number. We are following the same thing for all endorsements. A condition for signing up is, how can you help our charitable trust? So far the administrative cost of the trust is negligible. Whatever you give, goes straight to the patients.'

This is in addition to a contribution from his personal earnings. Having realized his worth, Khan is building on his Robin Hood-like image. Being Human T-shirts, his paintings, Being Human Productions (proceeds from films made under this banner are to be devoted completely to charity) and a chain of restaurants are on the anvil.

'Working in the industry, I can only raise that much, but with my name if I can endorse some stuff if they want me to, plus be a part of it then it adds up. There are times when they might want somebody else to endorse the product but still be a part of the charity, which is fine by me,' explains the star.

Understanding that one can leverage one's worth for the greater good is an important learning. Doing well by others is always seen as someone else's job but Khan's businesslike approach to charity has set an example, making it feasible at both macro and micro levels.

FAMILY AND FRIENDS THAT WORK TOGETHER, STAY TOGETHER

'A family in harmony will prosper in everything.'
—*CHINESE PROVERB*

One of the most interesting things about Khan is the tremendous goodwill he enjoys within the industry, regardless of his professional highs and lows. Everybody wants him for a friend. Most of his former girlfriends continue to remain friends with him, even turning to him occasionally for advice or assistance. And when such an occasion presents itself, he always lends a helping hand.

But it does not end there. All actresses, new or old, mainstream or otherwise, want to work with him, a fact he dismisses in a lighter vein. According to him, 'If there is even one flop, they will all run away!'

Khan's claim does not ring true. At a Being Human fashion show in 2010 almost every prominent actor from the industry

(Aamir Khan, Akshay Kumar, Ajay Devgn, Priyanka Chopra, Katrina Kaif, Bipasha Basu, Kareena and Karisma Kapoor) was on the ramp, showing solidarity with him.

He, in turn, is always there to help and support them. For instance, he agreed to perform a song for buddy Preity Zinta's film *Ishk in Paris* (2013). He also took friend Sanjay Dutt on board for *Bigg Boss* (2006–), a show that Khan was hosting on Colors channel.

'I prefer to work with people I get along with,' says Khan.

To Khan's credit, he is equally generous and supportive of newcomers as of his old acquaintances. In the early part of his career, Khan acted in Sanjay Leela Bhansali's first film *Khamoshi: The Musical* (1996), despite its risky subject of a deaf-mute couple and their musically inclined daughter. He has constantly encouraged and established young talent, including Arjun Kapoor and Himesh Reshammiya (who incidentally credits the superstar for establishing his career).

A generous heart is one that is loved by all, a quality that has helped Khan to a great extent. Those that he takes a shine to are happily included in his close circle of friends and family. Although all may not support his past actions, he is unanimously liked by most people within the film industry and outside it too.

FITNESS FUNDAS

'Take care of your body. It's the only place you have to live.'
—JIM ROHN

Among the anecdotes that I love to cite is one that epitomizes Khan's fitness regime. One day, while I was walking at Bandra Bandstand, a jogger (Khan) with two bouncers following, huffed past. It was an unusual sight, but not unexpected, given that Bandstand is the address for several film stars and city hotshots, including business tycoons. But what followed—a crowd of fans, jogging behind the star at a respectful distance all the way to his residence—was a memorable sight. Interestingly Khan, if he was perturbed by it, never let his feelings show. He continued with his run and went home only after he had finished the entire round.

If one is fortunate, one might just spot the superstar cycling to a film shoot. Khan was among the first actors in the industry—as early as the 1980s when he was a model in several television commercials—who could boast of a worked out, sculpted physique, displayed to advantage in countless films. So much so that it earned him the moniker of 'Shirtless Khan'! Not that his fans mind this exhibition the least bit.

Given that his physicality besides a brattish charm is such a vital part of Khan's superstar persona, being in shape is imperative. And even though he enjoys his biryani and other calorie-laden savouries, he is extremely particular about keeping up his fitness levels. That he can drop a size with just a couple of days of running helps his cause tremendously. During Khan's visit to Hyderabad for the Celebrity Cricket League tournament, guests at his hotel were in for a pleasant surprise—Salman Khan jogging about in the corridors as the gym was shut!

And quite like his other endeavours, generosity slips into Khan's fitness regimen as well. He has helped co-stars and potential competitors like Hrithik Roshan—who was then assisting his father Rakesh Roshan on *Karan Arjun* (1995)—with tips on beefing up his physique. Sonakshi Sinha, who was plump as a teenager, was also encouraged by Khan to shed weight and join the movies. Young actors like Arjun Kapoor have been at the receiving end of fitness advice from the star who has thrown open the doors of his personal gym for them.

A true master is one who imparts his secrets without fear that his student might surpass him. The generosity of a person can be truly measured by this single trait. In Khan's case he has a lot to lose with other younger stars outshining him in the physique department. But he still goes out of his way to help people who want to improve their fitness and physique.

BE YOURSELF

'Ride the energy of your own unique spirit.'—CABRIELLE ROTH

Given the love that surrounds him, it would be difficult not to point out the advantages of Being Salman. The superstar is keenly aware of it himself. Be it on television shows, in interviews or films, Khan is comfortable in his own skin, speaking his mind on various subjects, in a style uniquely his own. He spoke up for veteran actor Kamal Haasan when *Vishwaroopam* was under attack, praised Aamir for creating social awareness and even defended Shah Rukh Khan on *Bigg Boss*. He also complimented Shah Rukh on the runaway success of *Chennai Express*. He continues to be protective of women friends as he was with Katrina Kaif when he objected to a particular costume she was wearing in the film *Ek Tha Tiger*.

And in being his irreverent self, he has consolidated himself as a brand, making his personal style and bhai-speak rather fashionable.

He has, however, made it rather clear that he does not like answering questions about his personal relationships, especially the romantic ones, because he considers it disrespectful towards the elders and loved ones of the person concerned.

The actor, who used to flare up earlier under provocation, has eased up a lot in the last few years. He simply avoids situations that could turn controversial, like addressing large crowds, since eager fans unintentionally push women and children in their attempt to get close to him. In fact, he prefers to keep away from promoting films in towns where crowd control could get out of hand.

'It's one life yaar, whatever is there in my destiny will happen. You go through situations and come out, sometimes you get stuck. Life is one big story and you should have a superb story to tell,' he says of his roller-coaster life and the lessons he has learnt from it.

Donating money and taking the moral high ground is not necessarily charitable. Khan, though naturally disposed to helping those less privileged than him, has expanded his generosity by extending it to different people—fans, friends, family members or the needy—in different ways. Learning from experience and handling unwarranted situations brought on by his celebrity status in a style uniquely his own has further improved Khan's image and consolidated his goodwill.

GENEROSITY, SALMAN BHAI STYLE

Salman Khan's life is inspirational at several levels. He has turned around his career and image, surmounting tough circumstances. For starters, he's proved that it's not over till you accept that it's over. Unlike most people, while Khan never over-analyses, he remains a sharp judge of people. For instance, even though all actresses, young and old, are vying to act opposite him, he understands that it is only because his films are doing well. He does not insist on their inclusion in forthcoming films unless they are a good fit with the project. And while Khan maintains that he has not learnt anything (from his experiences), to attribute his second innings exclusively to luck would be inaccurate. The huge profits his films generate and his growing goodwill are obviously a result of his reworked Being Khan strategy!

☆ **Charity, handle with care:** Khan's charitable endeavours, because they suggest a genuine concern and involvement, have certainly worked wonders. But too much of a good thing and its reckless disbursement does not always deliver great results. Khan has recently institutionalized his charitable efforts through the Being Human Foundation for it to benefit a larger number of people. A clear segregation of work and charitable endeavours has helped him consolidate the charity, further strengthening his star power. The significant difference here is that Khan no longer makes charity a part of his creative decisions.

☆ **Find your groove:** Whether it is the atrocious grammar

of his tweets or his home-grown logic of what-will-be-will-be with a generous dose of the wicked wit, Khan, by being himself, is the perfect star package. While several actors consciously try to change their image, Khan remains happy in his groove. The superstar who always had a steady following among the small-town youth is now actively sought after by various political parties, NGOs and, of course, corporates to endorse their cause or product. Having understood his fan base, and the qualities that retain his top position, Khan has begun engaging more with his fans through his television shows, Twitter and press interviews, thus expanding his popularity.

His fans are happy to get a glimpse of the real Khan while studios are willing to bankroll anything featuring him. A win-win situation indeed!

☆ **A friend in need builds goodwill:** Though he no longer bases his professional choices—namely the movies he acts in—on charitable considerations, he has not stopped helping co-stars or colleagues.

Khan is always ready to make a guest appearance, as he did for Hema Malini's last directorial venture *Tell Me O Kkhuda* (2011). Or like the ones in *Baghban* (2003) and *Baabul* (2006), for director–producer Ravi Chopra. It earns him unstinted support from his peers. Khan also makes it a point to attend industry functions. With such goodwill around you, riding the storm becomes far easier.

☆ **Be involved with the work that you do:** Revisiting what worked for him, Khan, who has always had a flair for writing, now puts his experience in movies to good use, making suggestions to improve the quality of the film. Ever since *Maine Pyar Kiya*, his first film as a bonafide hero, Khan has enjoyed a steady following among the young, but later when his films flopped, he realized that stardom takes one only that far. It cannot compensate for shoddy concepts or mediocre work. Strong, personality-appropriate scripts are high priority with the superstar. Over the years Khan has realized the fact that stardom may come with luck, but it stays only with those who consistently work on it.

Acknowledgements

In the course of writing this book, my computer crashed twice. We also moved house. Among several temptations which beckoned, an invitation to the prestigious Berlin Film Festival had to be passed up. And then there were the official duties that most certainly could not be overlooked. In short, I had my work cut out. So it was with great relief and some trepidation that I sent off the manuscript and now, seeing it complete, I cannot help feeling deliriously happy. Having accomplished the task of putting the book together, the time has finally arrived to express a heartfelt gratitude to all those who lent a helping hand in my maiden venture.

The first thank you goes to my significant other Piyush, who made this book happen.

I owe Kapish Mehra much gratitude for having the foresight and faith to sign me up and not mincing his words when critiquing the first draft. It certainly helped.

Thanks to Farida Haider, whose suggestions and research were invaluable and ensured that I kept the deadline, K. Aishwarya for his illustrations and the Rupa editorial team for making the book read sharper.

A big round of thanks to my mother Rashmi Sinha for putting up with erratic phone calls and cheering me on in her own special way.

For my brother Prashant, Alok Uncle, my father Arvind Sinha, sister Priyamvada, my ma-in-law Shakuntala Jha, Tusshar and Stardust, who were incessantly badgered for feedback, this is a small token of my gratitude.

A special thank you goes out to Ajita and Abhijit who, despite their hectic schedule, painstakingly gave feedback at every stage of my writing.

Another special thank you to John Abraham and Amitabh Bachchan who have always been encouraging and supportive of all my endeavours.

And, last but not the least, heartfelt gratitude to the stars featured in this book for the insights they gave me over the years, and the film fraternity at large for their generosity.

References

Amitabh Bachchan
Screen, 10–16 April 2009
_____, 6–12 November 2009
_____, 17–23 June 2011
_____, 1–7 July 2011
_____, 18–24 May 2012
_____, 21–27 September 2012
_____, 12–18 October 2012
_____, 2–8 November 2012
_____, 21–27 June 2013

Shah Rukh Khan
Screen, 7–13 November 2008
_____, 8–14 October 2010
_____, 30 September–6 October 2011
_____, 16–22 November 2012

Vidya Balan
Screen, 17–23 April 2009
_____, 8–14 February 2013

Aamir Khan
The Guardian, 27 October 2002

Screen, 20–26 June 2008
____, 1–7 January 2010
____, 30 July–5 August 2010
____, 21–27 January 2011
____, 24–30 June 2011
____, 7–13 December 2012

Katrina Kaif
Salman Khan on Katrina Kaif—*Screen* Preview Coverage, 17–23 August 2012
Screen Preview Coverage, 17–23 August 2012
Screen, 12–18 December 2008
____, 17–23 May 2013

John Abraham
Screen, 2–8 January 2009
____, 29 October–5 November 2010
____, 22–28 February 2013

Ranbir Kapoor
Screen, 9–15 October 2009
____, 2–8 July 2010
TBIP Tête-à-Tête, thebigindianpicture.com, September 2012
Screen, 4–10 October 2013

Aishwarya Rai Bachchan
Screen, 6–12 November 2009
Rediff.com, 29 March 2000

Hrithik Roshan
Tere Mere Beach Mein, Star Plus, 26 September 2009

Screen, 14–20 May 2010
____, 28 January–3 February 2011
https://twitter.com/iHrithik
www.simigarewal.com

Karan Johar
Screen, 14–20 November 2008
____, 30 October–5 Nov 2009
____, 27 April–3 May 2012
Alia Bhatt on Karan Johar—*Screen* Preview Coverage, 19–25 October 2012
Kareena Kapoor on Karan Johar—*Screen*, 30 November–6 December 2012

Salman Khan
Screen, 22–28 August 2008
____, 22–28 January 2010
____, 10–16 September 2010
____, 26 August–1 September 2011
____, 10–16 August 2012
____, 15–21 June 2012
____, 21–27 December 2012

Made in the USA
Monee, IL
03 May 2026

49438690R00115